How to Be Happy on Mondays

Life Lessons To Acquire Wealth, Health, and Happiness Every Day of the Week

Enjoy!

Bruce McCombs

Bruce McCombs

ISBN: 978-1-944066-99-4

Library of Congress Control Number: 2022940266

For bulk purchases, speaking inquiries, and coaching programs with Bruce McCombs Enterprises, visit

https://bmcce.com/

For Mother Beverly

Contents

Acknowledgements

If I could offer one piece of advice to others, it would be to surround yourself with love. The content of our character is greatly affected by the care and kindness of the people who come in and out of our lives, especially those who want us to grow and succeed. They know our potential, mentor us, provide us with opportunity after opportunity, hold us accountable, believe in our dreams, and share in our happiness.

I have been blessed with much more than my share of such constant, competent, and visionary people to guide me along my path – even when I got lost, even when I wanted desperately to go in another direction, and even when the path looked like it wasn't leading anywhere great. They've loved me through it all.

It is my honor to introduce them to you.

My sister, Patricia McCombs, was a born rescuer. If you needed help, whether you realized it or not, she'd hold out her hand, smile your troubles away, and offer simple words of encouragement to let you know you could get through this. She was strong, especially when it came to saving herself and so many others from the throes of alcoholism. I can't help but think of her as the angel of Alcoholics Anonymous. I can't help but think of her as mine.

My older brother, Charles Herbert, who we also called Bubba, was the bravest person I knew. He was so much older that I didn't know him well, but what I did know stuck: he fought for his country during the Vietnam War, he took care of his family and friends, he fought ALS like a warrior, and he set the sky-high standard for how Patricia and I should treat our mother. He taught me some of my favorite lessons, including how to drive a car and how to play poker.

Growing up, I was blessed to have many friends from different walks of life, but no better friends than Chuck, Eddy, Louis, Rick, and Travis. Chuck is a multi-state racquetball champion, and a terrific golfer. Eddy plays poker for fun, and is the best in our circle of friends. Louis founded his own computer repair company. Rick earned his PhD. And Travis moved to Alaska to be a high school head football coach and enjoy the great outdoors. No matter how long it's been since we last talked, we always pick up right where we left off the last time. I wouldn't trade them for the world.

John, my first sales mentor, took an interest in me at CLR/Fast-Tax, and asked me if I wanted to join his sales organization and "Make some real money!" He shared opportunity and information freely with me, and I benefitted greatly from his generosity.

Matt, my manager at Oracle, recognized my performance, supported me, and shared all the best, most profitable accounts with me. Under his tutelage, I prospered and achieved beyond my wildest dreams.

I also wish to extend my gratitude to Susan, my Certified Professional Co-Active Coach (CPCC), who helped me change careers from Enterprise Sales to Performance Coaching. She emphasized the importance of values when deciding on a life shift of any kind, and challenged me to find something that gave me freedom and purpose.

A special thank you to Dr. Joe Verghese, Professor of Neurology & Medicine and Founding Director, Montefiore-Einstein Center for the Aging Brain, Albert Einstein College of Medicine, for pursuing the Movement Intervention for Memory Enhancement (MIME) study to determine if social dancing can slow the progress of cognitive decline. I am honored to contribute what I can to his endeavors.

My life is, in large part, a result of being Beverly Maxine Schutte's son. With such a loving, gracious, forgiving leader at the helm, I couldn't possibly steer wrong. But when I did veer off, she was there to listen and gently guide me back. Honestly, she was the best listener I have ever known, opening her heart on the spot, and listening to every word I had to say. "Stay humble and work harder than everyone else" was her lifelong motto, and I am lucky enough to have inherited it. I dedicate this book to her.

Last but certainly not least is my beautiful wife, Pamela, a living gift from God. I waited my whole life for her, and, boy, was she worth the wait. This book – and the rest of my life – are all for her.

About the Author

Bruce McCombs is a highly awarded enterprise sales coach, speaker, and author. His first book, *How to Become a $1 Million Enterprise Sales Leader*, is designed to improve a leader's performance and create wealth. While at Oracle, the world's second-largest software company, he earned over seven figures in sales for consecutive years, and elevated himself to become the number one sales leader worldwide. Equally impressive, Bruce sold $170 million in software and services during his Oracle career.

That wasn't enough. Through all of his successes and triumphs, he knew he was here for more. After leaving the tech industry, he switched careers, formed Bruce McCombs Enterprises, and became a Certified Professional Co-Active Coach (CPCC) and graduate of Co-Active Training Institute (CTI), the world's leading coaching organization.

Today, Bruce coaches sales leaders with his proprietary systems and methodology, and considers their successes his own. It is a wonderful way to pay back all of his own mentors. In addition, he regularly volunteers for the Small Business Administration, mentoring entrepreneurs to make better decisions to plan for their success, and is a seasoned veteran of Toastmasters International.

Perhaps his proudest accomplishment is creating The Beverly McCombs Foundation – Dance for Cognitive Enhancement. Since his mother's valiant ten-year battle with Alzheimer's, it is his passion to help discover all the ways dancing protects against the risk of cognitive decline.

Bruce is a proud graduate of the University of Texas in Austin, and balances his time between the Great State of Texas and his adopted California. If you can't find him, he's likely on a dance floor. He and his wife Pamela competed in ballroom dancing as amateurs, and they have won several Senior Latin ballroom dance championships. They live by Edward Lear's beautiful words: "Hand in hand, by the edge of the sand, they danced by the light of the moon."

Preface

I'm fortunate that I was struck by an epiphany at a few points in my life. Those moments when I experienced a stunning realization that I couldn't ignore – no matter how hard I tried – were the catalysts that allowed me to make great changes in my life. It is my hope for you that you hear those opportunities when they knock, and open your door to them. You'll find that they're the best guests of your life, but also the most demanding.

It's okay. They'll be worth it.

My epiphanies were tough, but they made sure that I knew that mine is not going to be a sad story. Read that again, and keep those words close; there may come a time in your own life when you'll need to repeat them to yourself. *This is not going to be a sad story.*

It's been a good reminder to myself as I record my memories, spending time in the sad parts of my life as well as the happiest, the difficult times and the easy days, and all the unforgettable moments in between that I'd almost forgotten.

Your lifetime should be the greatest story ever told. No matter where you begin or where you end, there may be a few chapters you'll want to skim, a few you'll want to read over and over again, and some that might make you put down the book altogether.

Keep going.

Write as many pages as you possibly can until the ink runs out.

Chapter One
You're Just Like Your Father

My life began in Dallas, Texas at Methodist Hospital early on Christmas morning, which is a fitting date since I've always considered myself one of my mother's best gifts. I'm sure she and my siblings would wholeheartedly agree if they were still here with us, but you'll just have to take my word for it.

I was the youngest of three children: Charles Herbert (C.H.), named after my maternal grandfather, was 13 years older, and Patricia was just two years old when I arrived. It must have been a tumultuous beginning, as my parents divorced two years after my birth. I never really knew a childhood *with* my father, so I can't truthfully tell you he was missed by me. I only know that I saw from a very early age how hard my mother worked to make a good life for us all. Of course, it's never been an easy task for a single woman to single-handedly take care of three children on her own, so we had to move in with my mother's parents to make ends meet when my parents split.

My grandfather, Charles Herbert (C.H.) Schutte, married my grandmother, Amelia Agnes Umsheid, in Galveston, Texas in 1908 when they were both 18 years old. They met in Galveston's large German community that still exists today, and shared many of the strict, disciplined, and driven characteristics for which their culture is admired. (Not by a wild, young boy like I was at the time, but my appreciation certainly grew as I did.)

My grandfather accepted a job with the Katy railroad after they married, and they moved to San Antonio to start their life together. He was later transferred to Dallas to manage the real estate division of the company. My grandmother, stayed home and maintained the house and her family, which eventually included her adult daughter and grandchildren. That couldn't have been easy.

Once in Dallas, my grandparents built a new house in Kessler Park, which is in Oak Cliff, Texas. It was – and still is – an amazing location, only two miles southwest of Downtown Dallas separated by the Trinity River. Their house was approximately 2,200 sq. ft. spread over nine rooms, and it cost $35,000 for them to build in 1931. Today, that house is appraised at over $800,000.

I loved that house, and its beautiful, convenient location. Kessler Park – named after George Kessler, a prominent and prescient real estate developer who had a gift for planning lasting communities – enjoys a topography of rolling hills and stunning tree lines, including many, many oaks, which is how Oak Cliff earned its name. It was an easy, idyllic setting for a childhood that wasn't always easy or idyllic.

My mother was a daddy's girl growing up and admired her father very much. Since she was an only child, she received a lot of undivided attention. Grandaddy was able to take the family on many vacations working for the railroad, across the USA, Canada, and Mexico. Her father also served as President of my mother's high school PTA. Knowing how his daughter loved to play tennis, Grandaddy helped raise enough money to build two tennis courts next to Sunset High, the school she attended. I take a lot of comfort in the fact that my mother received this type of love from the first male figure in her life, as it makes my heart break a little less for what she must've endured later with my father.

My grandfather used to play golf a few blocks from the house at a municipal golf course called Stevens Park. Growing up, me and my friends played it, too, but we called the course Beautiful Stevie because it's nestled in such a gorgeous area. I find inexplicable joy in the knowledge that Grandaddy was a pretty good golfer and also enjoyed playing tennis. For some reason, I love the idea of him having leisure time and filling it with sport; it makes me feel close to him to this day that we shared a love of fitness. I never got to know him because he suffered a heart attack and made his transition when I was three years old, but one of my earliest and best memories was accompanying him to the 7-Eleven where he'd buy us fudgesicles, a memory that still keeps me warm.

Memories of my grandmother, however, do not have the same effect. When we moved in with her and my grandfather, she took on the role of disciplinarian when my mother was at work. It was necessary, I'm told, because I was a trying young boy. I climbed when I should've stayed on the ground, touched when I should've kept my hands to myself, ran when I should've walked a bit more carefully, and talked back when I should've simply responded, "Yes, ma'am."

We called her Mommy because she was very much like our second mother while our own worked three jobs to support us. Since my grandfather wasn't around anymore, and my father was long gone, it was left to my mother and Mommy to discipline me. Whenever my mom finally walked through the door at the end of a long day, physically and mentally exhausted, Mommy let her know every unruly thing I'd done in her absence. *In detail.*

My grandmother's favorite way to stop me in my tracks was to tell me – in words overflowing with resentment and unfiltered anger – that my actions reminded her of the lowest human on earth: my father.

"You're just like Bill McCombs," she'd say, shaking her head disgustedly. She rightly despised the man because of how he treated her daughter and then abandoned her grandchildren, leaving my mom to care for two kids and working herself to death to barely pay the bills.

> *The hurt that troubled children create is never greater than the hurt they feel.*
>
> **L. Tobin**

Every single time I'd hear those words, my emotions went into overdrive. Straight away, an almost uncontrollable anger filled my body and I'd literally shake to keep it all inside. Then, when the moment was over and I was left alone with my thoughts and anticipated punishment, I'd feel the shame of being connected by blood and behavior to this vile person. I thought I was mad at my grandmother, but it was only later that I realized I was mad at my situation.

My grandmother couldn't take care of us every day, so my mom enrolled me and Patricia in a nearby nursery school. She'd drop us off before heading to work, and pick us up on her way home. It was an exhausting schedule for all of us, I'm sure.

It wasn't always hard. There was joy, I know, because I remember it clearly. There were moments when my mother danced, for instance, when she transformed in front of our eyes from an overworked single parent trying to make ends meet into a young ingenue whose only care in the world was perfecting her promenade hesitation. She was a wonder.

She wanted us to enjoy dance, too, so she enrolled us in dance classes: Patricia took ballet, and I learned how to tap. We performed at our dance school recitals, with my mother beaming proudly from the audience, leaning forward in her seat as if she wished she was up there with us. I kept a photo she took of me up on stage with a few other guys dressed up in bear costumes. I, of course, lost my bear cap along the way; it must've been hot, or I'd had enough of the costume!

I didn't mind performing in front of an audience, and I never got nervous like some of the other kids. I'd hear them telling their parents, "No! I don't want to!" Maybe I didn't want to, either, but I'd sure never say that to my mother.

When I was very young, she got me on a kids' show called Romper Room. Do you remember that program? Every episode began with the Pledge of Allegiance and then it was time for games, exercise, songs, stories, and moral lessons. There was a character called Mr. Do-Bee who dressed up as a giant bumblebee and taught us kids about right and wrong behavior, and also a naughty alter ego known as Mr. Don't-Bee. They'd start their sentences with "Do bee good citizens!" or "Don't bee disrespectful to your parents!" My favorite part was when they served milk and cookies to the kids on air, and everyone recited the Romper Room prayer: "God is great, God is good, Let us thank Him for our food. Amen."

My appearance on Romper Room was not as epic as I hoped it would be, as the camera caught me sucking my thumb and I had to deal with snide remarks from the older kids at nursery school for a while. It could've been worse! Thank goodness it happened well before iPhones and social media, or I would've become a viral meme.

My older brother, C.H., escaped these dance lessons and little adventures, as he was so much older than me and Patricia. I remember looking up to him in so many ways. Early on, he put up a basketball hoop above my grandparents' garage with a backboard he made himself out of two-inch plywood. I started by watching him shoot buckets, learning from his moves, until I was old enough and tall enough to make my own shots. I could stay in the driveway for hours at a time, pretending I had an NBA arena full of cheering fans who all knew my name. Some days, I was Casey Russell. Others, I was Elgin Baylor. But most days, I was just happy to share that makeshift court with my brother.

I didn't see him very often because Bubba – as we called him – was pretty much a grown man. That's how it worked with 17- and 18-year olds; once they graduated from high school, they moved out and lived on their own. I'm sure he was having the time of his life.

C.H. was about six feet tall, thin, and good looking. He had a crew cut and thick beard, but was usually clean shaven, and he always, always dressed well. I don't recall where Bubba lived. Isn't that funny? Back then, we didn't know everyone's whereabouts like we do today. Sometimes, we went weeks without seeing or hearing from him. But then we'd hear the unmistakable roar of his motorcycle and knew he'd come to check on Mom.

He also checked in from time to time to make sure I was behaving. When he heard news to the contrary, he'd find a wire coat hanger and chase me around, threatening to spank me with it. I always knew he was kind of kidding, but I also knew that if I really misbehaved for our mom and grandmother, he'd make good on his threats. That possibility always put the fear of God in me! C.H. knew Mom didn't have the stamina to constantly discipline me with her hectic work schedule, and absolutely no free time to take care of herself and her own needs. Hence, he dished out some strong attitude adjustment when I misbehaved.

There wasn't a time in my life when I didn't seek his approval, or learn from his actions. For example, I never witnessed him judge other people for the way they looked, how they talked, or the color of their skin. He treated everyone with the same level of respect and consideration.

As for his relationship with my mother, it was textbook of how a son should behave. He openly appreciated her efforts and hard work, he never failed to address her as ma'am, and he always opened doors for her. He was a gentleman, through and through, and she must've been so proud that he belonged to her and that she'd raised him well. Did I mention he always held her hand? That little act threw me a little because I never offered that same type of affection toward my mother when I was growing up. It's as though there wasn't the time or the space to tell each other "I love you" in those days, in between her working, competing in a man's world, and then being forced to come home to discipline me. I'm sure it was important for Mom to show strength as the dominant figure in our household, to make up for the lack of a father figure.

> *"Heavy is the head, forced to wear two crowns."*
>
> **R.P. Falconer**

That's not to say my mother and I weren't close. We were. With only two bedrooms in my grandmother's house – the third was rented out to raise additional, much needed income – we were forced to bunk together. Patricia was my grandmother's roommate, and I stayed with my mom. We all had our own beds, but there wasn't a lot of privacy. I didn't care; it was reassuring to wake up and see my mom in the next bed. I always felt safe, and I believe this early living arrangement enabled me to be closer to my mom as I got older, and shaped our relationship throughout adulthood.

My whole life changed when my grandmother informed us that she was selling the house. It was too much, she told us, even with her social security and the money my grandfather had left her in his estate. Selling the family home would give her enough money to live comfortably and without worry for the rest of her life. It must have been emotional for my grandmother to leave the home she and my grandfather built, but I also knew she would relish the fact that I'd no longer be underfoot. Whether it was reality or not, she never seemed to take a liking to me, and I took that to heart.

Maybe I am just like my deadbeat father, I'd think to myself, embedding that belief deep in my psyche without really realizing it.

Ultimately, my grandmother's decision made sense to me, and I wasn't worried about what would come next for us. The only thing I'd ever known is that my mom had never let us down before, and I knew she would continue to do everything in her power and beyond to make sure our lives remained stable and happy. Plus, I was secretly glad to put some distance between me and my grandmother.

Chapter Two
Life Goes On

We moved to a new apartment complex a couple of miles from where we were living. Since my family was devout Catholic, Mom enrolled us in St Cecilia's elementary school a block away from our new home. The girls dressed in plaid skirts, white blouses, and green sweaters, and the boys wore gray slacks with crisp white shirts. Morning Mass was mandatory every weekday, then came the Pledge of Allegiance, and then – without fail – my first-grade teacher started her daily chase after me with a ruler in her hands, ready to smack my knuckles until I stopped misbehaving. Ahh, Sister Mary Ann. She reminded me so much of my grandmother – short and stout, looking on me with a disapproving look behind wire-rimmed glasses – and, in fact, she picked up where my grandmother left off. She probably didn't deserve my blatant disregard for her classroom rules, but I'd been raised in a household of strong, vocal women, and her loud and constant reprimands didn't faze me one bit.

I was excited when my First Communion rolled around. The Catholic Church determined that seven- and eight-year olds were ready to participate in this rite of passage, and I couldn't be happier when I finally reached the age of reason. Every Mass up to that point, I'd have to either wait in my pew while everyone marched slowly to the altar to enjoy the body and blood of Christ, or I'd tag along with my mother to receive a boring old blessing from the priest.

At our church, we were able to choose a holy name we'd like to use throughout our Catholic journey, one that would inspire us while accepting the sacraments. I chose the name Christopher simply because I liked it, never equating him with the patron saint of travelers. Now, I chuckle whenever I see a car passing with St. Christopher's image hanging from the rear view mirror. I'd like to think I knew back then that I'd be going places, but that might be a stretch.

One of the most important parts of our Catholic training was confession. It sounds simple enough: enter a closet-sized dark booth, kneel down, wait for the priest to open the screen between his section and yours, tell him *most* of your sins for the week, get a stern reprimand, say a few Hail Marys and Our Fathers as penance, and you're clear.

Even though I got into trouble daily, there wasn't much to tell the priest beyond, "I talked back to my grandmother" or "I had to be told a few times to take out the trash." Still, I was incredibly nervous before my first confession. I forced myself into the confessional, felt a wave of claustrophobia, and knelt down. As soon as the screen slid open, I stumbled through my prepared words – "Bless me, Father, for I have sinned." – and then panicked that I'd done it all wrong and peed my pants.

Now, this was no small accident. The urine dripped down my pants, onto the floor, under the confessional door, and into the hallway. I froze. I couldn't *believe* this was happening to me. And as much as I didn't want to be in this cramped, confined space, I also couldn't imagine the ridicule that was waiting for me outside of it. I didn't say a word to the priest, and finished my confession. When I exited, I tried to cover the wet stain on the front of my pants as best I could with my hands, but my hands weren't nearly big enough.

A giant's hands wouldn't have been big enough.

At first no one noticed. But when we walked outside, the bright sunlight was like a spotlight on the wet spot.

"What's that?" someone asked, and then it seemed like the whole world started laughing. I was mortified, especially since I was the only one who freaked out in the confessional. A kid named Paul began bullying me from that day on, starting a real fight a few days later with punches and everything. Unfortunately, I got pummeled that day because Paul was twice my size. Even more unfortunately, that was not the last fisticuffs in which I was involved. The only good news is that I eventually grew in more ways than one, and very few of my peers picked on me.

At that age, my entire world revolved around school, my classmates, pretending to be Jim Brown in any pick-up football games I could find, and getting home in time for dinner. I loved our new apartment and I loved my surroundings. It was a simple, satisfying, small life.

But then came November 22, 1963. I was at school, hunting for a book in the library, when our principal's voice came over the school intercom. Her name was Sister Benita Frances, and like most of the nuns I'd met during my church and school career, she was as no-nonsense and stoic as they came. But her voice caught on the news she had to share with us, and I knew she was trying not to cry.

"President Kennedy has been shot."

Unlike Sister Benita Frances, my classmates and I didn't even try to hold in our tears.

It was a horrible time in our history, and an even worse time to be a resident of Dallas. The whole world was mad at us; the headlines in every newspaper from Paris to Papua New Guinea might as well have read "Dallas killed President Kennedy!"

We left school early that day. I'm sure every family in the US was in front of their televisions, trying to learn all the devastating details. President Kennedy was shot by Lee Harvey Oswald, a guy who lived only three miles east of our home. Police ended up capturing Oswald at the Texas Theater on Jefferson Avenue in downtown Oak Cliff – our area! We knew all the business and retail storefronts that Oswald ran through before he was captured, and Patricia and I saw a movie at that theater just two days before the assassination!

It was all way too close for comfort.

"Things turn out best for the people who make the best out of the way things turn out."

John Wooden

By the time I reached the sixth grade, I'd moved from the only home I'd ever known into an apartment, my older brother went off to join the Navy, and now I was told I'd be switching schools. That meant new friends, new teachers, and new stresses. I'd had more than enough lessons in the old adage *Life Goes On* for my liking, but I did my best to adapt.

My mother decided to terminate our school contract with St. Cecilia, determining I was prepared for public school. Her feeling may have been that I'd spent my early, formative years in a religious environment, but it was now time to spread my wings a bit. Money was tight, after all, and the tuition was likely prohibitive.

My new school happened to be across the street from St. Cecilia's, so I was familiar with the area. I'd met a couple of guys my age at our apartment complex who would be in my grade, so that was a relief. They, too, grew up without fathers in their lives, and their mothers shared a lot of the same characteristics with mine: strong, determined, and ready to get to work. We all knew we had very little leeway in terms of bad behavior because our moms would wreak havoc on our lives. I'm grateful for that accountability, especially as I've learned how much attention and patience it took my mother to achieve that level of respect from a growing, trying boy.

Louis and Eddy were my first friends at my new school. Although Louis was not Catholic, he still attended St. Cecilia on Sundays. Mixing an hour-long Latin Mass with young boys who would rather be running around outside is a recipe for disaster. My apologies to anyone sitting in the back of the church who were alarmed by the unusual noises coming from our pew. I'm certain my friends would send theirs, as well.

It's always been my preference to be outside, spending my time doing something enjoyable. Even at the young age, I knew I was fortunate that Dallas weather allowed me the freedom to grab a light jacket, yell goodbye to my mother or Patricia, and race out to play...anything. If there was a game going on, I wanted to be on one of the teams.

> *"Do you know what my favorite part of the game is? The opportunity to play."*
>
> **Mike Singletary**

Growing up in my grandparents' house, I started scrimmaging by myself, setting up a field of sorts between the driveways and walkways between my neighbors' houses. My knees and elbows didn't stand a chance with all that concrete! At the end of every point I scored on myself, I'd kick a field goal between the neighbor's trees. It was a wonder they never said a word to my grandmother about me trampling their plants and breaking all sorts of branches. I must've known I was playing on shaky ground because I started mowing their lawns for free!

I also played baseball in a vacant lot five houses down from Mommy's house. Before each game, Patricia and I mowed the knee-deep grass so the field would look like an official baseball diamond. We cut the grass outlining the base path short, and left the infield and outfield grass a little longer – just like in the big leagues.

When I hit the sixth grade, we'd play softball before school on a dirt playing field so close that St. Cecelia was visible from home plate. On my very first attempt at bat, I hit the ball over the fence and into the street, impressing my new classmates and enhancing my reputation.

"You should play for the school softball team!" they told me. I had to decline, though, because I was already playing for a Little League team and there just wasn't enough time to do everything.

These days in my childhood were as close to perfect as I could imagine. All the neighborhood kids started gathering around noon on Saturdays for the first pitch – after cartoons and chores – and we'd play until we had to go home for dinner. If we hit the ball into the street, cars stopped. The neighbors were very aware of our presence, and seemed to enjoy the fact that we were all playing together.

When we got a little older, we took our game to Burnett Field a few miles away. This was no empty lot maintained by me and Patricia! No, sir. Dallas' minor league team played at Burnett, and it seated roughly 12,000 spectators. Fortunately for us, Burnett's security was nonexistent, and we snuck in easily. Now, that was an experience. We pretended that we were the Yankees and the Dodgers playing in the World Series. I was Mickey Mantle and one of my friends was Sandy Koufax, the famous pitcher for the LA Dodgers.

In between, I played shortstop for the Little League Roundtables, a team well known in the 12-14 age group throughout Dallas. My batting average was .375, making me one of the best players who consistently made the All-Star team every year.

"A trophy carries dust. A memory lasts forever."

Mary Lou Retton

All athletes have fond memories of specific plays they made, and I'm no exception. I once stopped a screaming hit from the batter by dropping to my knees so the ball would not go through my legs, then throwing out the runner at first base, all while still on my knees. At that point in the game, there were two outs and runners on second and third, so it was a big play. That effort helped us win the game three-to-two and secure a place in the playoffs!

During the fall, I played halfback for a team in the Pop Warner football league called the Little Cowboys. Although I was better at baseball, I preferred the gridiron sport because I had good size for my age, speed, and agility, and thought I would grow big enough to play college football.

The seventh game of the year, we played the Jets on Halloween night. They were dressed in black with orange trim and orange numbers, and we were outfitted in Dallas Cowboys-esque blue jerseys and white pants. They had a running back named Tommy – we knew this because all the cheers coming from the stands were "Tommy! Tommy! Tommy!" – who dominated the game, rushing for more yards than I can remember and scoring at least three touchdowns. He was a beast. We lost that game without scoring any points, but we ended with good team stats of eight wins and only two losses. Once the season was over, I tended not to worry about what *was* and shifted my mindset to what *could be*; I made a list of the skills I needed to improve, and I'd work until my weaknesses were strengths.

Oh, I could fill these pages with plays I made and the ones I missed, and there will be a few more that I don't want to forget. But the most important part about this time in my life was the support of my mother.

I've heard many stories about parents getting upset if their kids weren't given starting positions on their teams or seeing enough playing time for their liking, but that wasn't my mom's style. No matter what I was doing, she was there. And the look I saw on her face when I found her in the stands or in the audience or on the sidelines made me feel so proud of myself. Loved. Like I could do anything and become someone of consequence.

She was my biggest fan. If there was a mom lottery, I won it.

Chapter Three
The Beatles Were Correct

My older sister, Patricia, loved The Beatles. She loved all music, really, but she was a true fanatic about John, Paul, George, and Ringo. If she was washing the dishes, she was singing "All you need is love!" Same if she was tidying up the living room, working on her homework, or brushing her teeth before bed.

It was hard to stay mad at Patricia, even when she was bossing me around, because I knew The Beatles' lyrics were coming.

"All you need is love! Love! Love! Love is all you need!" She'd even add in the trumpet sounds.

As her luck would have it, The Beatles came to Dallas for a concert on September 18, 1964. You should've heard my sister's power of persuasion, using every tactic in the book to convince our mother that we *had* to go see them.

"No way!" I objected. "I don't want to miss football practice for a concert! And I don't even like The Beatles!"

That was a lie. I loved The Beatles. They were my favorite group at the time, and *Day Tripper* was my favorite song. I was also partial to *All You Need is Love*, but that one belonged to Patricia.

The day of the concert, we piled into the car and made our way to the arena. The lot was packed with cars and excited fans, and we drove around for a while trying to find a spot. We got to the end of yet another crowded row and almost ran smack into a limo. My sister and mother and I all gasped at the near miss, and then looked more closely. Behind the shocked limo driver were four equally shocked faces: John, Paul, George, and Ringo! Of course, my sister went bananas, screaming and crying while my mother and I rolled our eyes at each other. Still, I must admit, it was kind of exciting to be *that* close to The Beatles.

That was honestly the most fun of the night, since we couldn't exactly hear the band play; the audience, made up mostly of over-excited young girls, screamed the entire concert and drowned out The Beatles altogether! It certainly didn't matter to my sister, though. Paying five dollars apiece to barely hear thirty minutes of The Beatles was worth it to her.

And from that moment on, I knew that music would be one of the great loves of my life.

The very next day, armed with all of our combined allowance money we'd been saving, Patricia and I marched right into the music store and bought a microphone, amplifier, and snare drum plus a music book that contained the words to The Beatles' and The Rolling Stones' songs. And then we went home and started practicing for our rock star life.

> *"It's all in the mind."*
>
> **George Harrison**

Oh, if only my living room mirror could tell this part of the story. I have to smile when I think of all the moves I tried out, the voice I'd try to make a little deeper, and the words I forgot. That's the beauty of youth, isn't it? I believed everything was possible, which was a fine change from only believing my grandmother's assessment of me: "You're just like your father."

My mirror disagreed with her: I was just like John Lennon and Mick Jagger.

In the seventh grade, I got a few friends together and started a band. We called ourselves The Dimensions, and practiced in my buddy Steve's garage. Steve played bass, Dudley lead guitar, and Chris was our drummer. The summer before we formed our band, I threatened to cut off Chris' long hair that he'd grown down past his shoulders! Thank goodness I didn't because that long hair gave our band some serious street credibility, and we became really good friends.

I was the lead singer, played some guitar, and was the primary promoter of the band. For our very first public performance, I signed us up for the school talent show. We were all pretty nervous before we went onstage, but my dance recital training kicked in and I gave the other guys a few words of advice that bolstered their confidence. What I didn't tell them is that there was no way I'd go out like I had on Romper Room. We *had* to do well!

We won that talent competition, so I'd say we did well. Our repertoire was entirely covers popular at the time: *Gloria* by Van Morrison, *House of the Rising Suns* by The Animals, *Satisfaction* by The Stones, and three songs from The Beatles, including *Day Tripper*. After that, we were asked to play for our seventh-grade music teacher's faculty party, a couple of county fairs, charity events, and more. The Dimensions enjoyed enough success that we stayed together until we entered junior high.

But life wasn't all perfect notes and standing ovations. Like I mentioned, my older brother, Bubba, had been uncertain about what he wanted to do after high school and ended up joining the Navy, serving his first tour on an aircraft carrier patrolling the Pacific. He came home on one of his scheduled leaves and happened to meet a young Catholic girl named Sandra. Back then, religion was one of the first hurdles a young couple had to jump; parents' approval came quicker if the chosen partner shared their faith. And so, with only six months left on his two-year Naval commitment, Bubba and Sandra decided to get married as soon as he was finished.

> *"The more I see, the less I know for sure."*
>
> **John Lennon**

Sandra was stunning, and I was really proud of my brother for choosing someone who liked kissing as much as Sandra seemed to like kissing. (Disclaimer: I was a little kid and caught them making out when she came over, but that memory stuck. I couldn't wait to grow up and find someone to kiss, too!) Unfortunately, I was too young to attend their wedding, but Patricia got to be the main flower girl and she never let me forget that I'd missed a very good party.

My brother and Sandra started their family quickly, and named their first child Timothy. Tammy and Todd followed soon after to fill out their beautiful family of five. I always looked up to Bubba, and seeing him with his wife and the children they made together filled me with even more admiration.

After the kids were born, C.H. partnered with a friend and opened a liquor store just south of downtown Dallas. He worked hard for every dime he earned. And then one day he got an out-of-the-blue call from a friend who'd served alongside Bubba, who told him that he was re-enlisting. The government increased the pay substantially for families and their dependents, and were offering more money under the GI Bill for veterans to get a college education after their service was completed. Bubba was still young enough and wanted to get his degree, so he sold his share in the liquor business to his partner and re-enlisted for his second two-year tour.

The Vietnam War began one year into it, and Bubba was shipped off to patrol the South China Sea. That's when the trouble started.

> *"War is over. If you want it."*
>
> **John Lennon**

He started experiencing muscle spasms and weird twitches, and there were moments when his speech was slurred a bit. The Navy sent him back to the US for testing, and the doctor diagnosed him with Amyotrophic Lateral Sclerosis (ALS), a neurodegenerative disease which causes the nervous system to slowly deteriorate, thus causing the person to lose their muscle strength and motor skills. Typically, ALS leads to death within three to five years, usually because the lungs fail when the neurons that send instructions to the respiratory system stop working. ALS is a rare disease, striking about five in every 100,000 people, and only affects some 350,000 people worldwide. We knew it as Lou Gehrig's disease, named after the great New York Yankee baseball player who died of ALS in 1941. And we knew it as a death sentence since there were no cures, something that crushes my heart to this day when I think of my big, strong brother knowing that fact, too.

The Navy physicians had no explanation how Bubba may have gotten the disease. We thought it might be genetic, but there was no history of nervous system disorders in his family tree. After an in-depth investigation, we concluded that it was probably an environmental after-effect from when he served in the war, but we couldn't prove it.

Unfortunately, Sandra decided that she did not want to be her husband's caretaker during his struggle with ALS, and asked him to move out. I don't know all the details that surrounded the decision, but I do know that it broke my mother's heart. Her only option was to bring Bubba home so she could care for him full-time.

Bubba settled into the house quickly. It felt like old times at first. I got my brother back, and although he was little slower this time around, he could still walk around and drive a car. Also different in our relationship was that we no longer played basketball together, but we did have a new hobby: poker.

Man, did Bubba love to play poker. He attended a set game every Wednesday, and I accompanied him as soon as I got home from school just in case anything unusual happened and he needed my assistance. There were usually six to seven guys playing Texas Hold 'Em and Five- and Seven-Card Stud. I'd sit behind Bubba, never saying a word, just listening to the conversations about the Navy, sports teams, and women. I got to know a side of my brother I'd missed because of our vast age difference, and I learned that Bubba was very much loved by his friends. It was the best education of my life.

Within three months, his disease became so pervasive and debilitating that Bubba could no longer drive himself to poker games. That made him mad, but there was no way he was missing Wednesday poker.

"You can drive me," he informed me in no uncertain terms. Although I was only 13 at the time, he knew that I knew how to drive. After all, he'd taught me himself a year prior with his own Ford Fairlane in the church parking lot across the street from where we lived.

We kept the driving arrangement a secret; my mom could not find out I was driving him or else she'd put a stop to poker. Even at my young age, I knew the stakes were high. My brother already had enough happiness stolen from him, and there was no way I'd be the one responsible for taking away his beloved poker games.

Within 18 months, the ALS had spread throughout his entire body, his muscles atrophied, and he lost the majority of his motor skills. He was now confined to a bed and his speech was severely impaired. When he spoke, he slurred his words, so it was difficult to understand what he was saying. To hear better, we leaned over so he could whisper in our ear. Charles' bodily function deteriorated to the point that mother was forced to admit him into the hospital for 24-hour care. This slow, anguishing death was tearing Mom apart, but she never let Bubba or the rest of us see her crack.

After two years of fighting ALS, Bubba died on December 31st, New Year's Eve, a date with much significance. I often wonder if he didn't leave then so our mother wouldn't have to endure another year of torture.

> *"Close your eyes and I'll kiss you. Tomorrow, I'll miss you."*
>
> **Paul McCartney**

Our entire family went to Veteran's Hospital that morning, a fitting cold, damp, and cloudy day. I saw Bubba lying on the bed, his skin discolored, his body stiff and lifeless. His eyes were closed, and mouth was open. After years of fighting, he finally looked peaceful. This was the first time I'd ever seen death, and I was surprised by its quiet hush and the emotions it brought out in me.

I wept for him then, and I also cried for my mother as she lost her oldest child. Her marriage didn't work out, as you already know, so perhaps C.H. was truly her first love. I think Bubba's death might have been the first time I learned how much love hurts.

His funeral was held at Calvary Hill Memorial Crematorium and Cemetery, which is operated by the Dallas Catholic diocese. In 1935, our grandfather had bought six plots next to each other for the family, so Bubba was laid to rest next to him. As customary for a veteran, the casket was draped in the American flag. As it was lowered, Father Vogel, our parish priest and close family friend, gave him his last rights

Everyone in Bubba's life attended – even Sandra. I sat next to his oldest son during the internment, but he was still so young and only understood that his father was gone but that he had so many friends. I guess that's all he needed to know. We wouldn't see Bubba's kids much after that, until the time when we never saw them again.

Try as I might, I can't find fitting words to describe the day other than it was incredibly sad. My brother was only 27 when he died, and I'd give anything for him to have had an easier, happier life. Anything.

In 2000, the US government released information that Vietnam and Gulf War vets had an unusually high number of confirmed cases of nervous disorder diseases like my brother's ALS. The speculation was that those servicemen who encountered chemical agents sprayed in Vietnam were most likely to be affected. As this news came 33 years after Bubba's death, it was difficult to prove the link between his ALS and his Vietnam tour of duty. If he was on a ship, how and when did he encounter chemical agents? It certainly would have been helpful to know more about Bubba's experience during his time in the military, but like most veterans of that generation, he was pretty tight-lipped about the difficult parts of his life. He literally took the information we needed to the grave.

We probably should have pressed the government harder at the time of his transition to get an answer, but we didn't think our own government could be responsible for our brother's death.

Or could it?

> *"One thing you can't hide –*
> *is when you're crippled inside."*
>
> **John Lennon**

I have very fond memories of my brother, but I harbor some guilt about the way I treated him when he got sick. I was insensitive more often than I'd like to admit, and I'm not sure why. Maybe I didn't like the way he got all my mother's attention, maybe I was finally letting out all the anger I'd built up from my tumultuous relationship with my grandmother...or maybe I was suddenly understanding that the only father figure I'd ever known was dying in front of my eyes, and I didn't want to feel that gutting abandonment twice.

Whatever the reasons, none were good enough. I hope he forgives me. And I hope, in the end, he only remembers me driving him to poker on Wednesday afternoons.

Chapter Four
"Are You Bruce McCombs?"

Take it from me: you never really want to hear a group of tough guys ripe for a fight ask if your name is, in fact, your name. For some reason, my youth was full of conversations that started like this; while I normally didn't initiate them, I always tried to finish them strong.

I've already told you about the first fight with a kid named Paul after my wet and not-so-wonderful holy confession, but I didn't tell you that it really left a mark on me. Beyond the black eye and fat lip left over from that day, I learned to always watch for cheap shots and – maybe more importantly and more useful – I also learned that there are people in life who want to hurt you.

> *"Hurt people hurt you."*
>
> **Charles Eads**

As the seventh grade school year came to an end, my classmates and I were really looking forward to Field Day. Even though the weather was hot and sticky by that time, we got to come to school in sporty clothes – along with the knowledge that most of the school day would be spent outside – which put us all in fantastic moods. There were races and other track and field events, softball, basketball, and any other competition the teachers organized. I was hyped to participate in as many as I was allowed.

Just before the start of my 100-yard dash, I noticed several older boys getting out of cars and walking toward...well...me. They were making direct eye contact with...well...me. I didn't know any of them, and I really couldn't imagine a scenario where older kids who could drive would come to a seventh grade school event in broad daylight with tons of teachers and parents in attendance and pick a fight with a much younger kid, so I just ran my race. Afterwards, as I walked toward the gym to change clothes, one of those older boys yelled out, "Are you Bruce McCombs?"

Uh oh.

"I am," I responded, my heart thumping in my throat.

"Yeah?" he sneered. "Well, my little brother John told me you like to act like a tough guy, and I'm here to see just how tough you are."

Between us, I was not feeling very tough at the moment, but I instinctively knew that this was one of those moments I just had to lean into. I remembered John. We played football against each other when I was on the Little Cowboys Pop Warner football team. There was one occasion when John tackled me by intentionally pulling on my facemask, dragging me to the ground. I got mad, and rightfully so; he could've seriously hurt me, and I didn't want him doing that to me or to my teammates ever again. I challenged him afterwards, and I guess I made him look bad in front of everyone. Whether he deserved that embarrassment or not, he hung onto his feelings and must've told his older brother about it. And now, here we were, six months later.

There were at least twenty older kids circled around him and me, encouraging him to start the fight, and I was scared out of my mind. Still, I shrugged and put up my fists. There are some fights you can talk through, and some you simply have to fight through; this seemed like a clear case of the latter option.

Fortunately, Mr. Fieldgold, the school principal, intervened before the first punch was thrown and stopped the fight. He ordered the older boys to leave campus or else he was going to call the police. They all left, but that was not the end of John's hurt feelings.

Before the start of eighth grade, we practiced football in the summer to prepare for the upcoming fall season. Coaches could not be present by league rule, and no formal training could be conducted, including summer football camps. But I'd been scrimmaging every summer wherever and whenever I could get a game going, whether that meant gathering up all the neighborhood kids or playing against myself in my neighbors' front yards. I knew exactly how to get around the rule.

"Meet me at the junior high school football field," I'd tell a few teammates, asking them to spread the word. Before long, we had regular and well-attended practices and pick up football games happening during the hottest hours of the Dallas summer days.

Boy, those practices were fun. No coaches yelling at us, no boring drills, no set agenda we were forced to follow – it was just pure fun and imagination. I designed more intricate plays as quarterback during those summer sessions than I'd likely ever use during a real game, and everyone else pushed their own limits, too. I've used those memories as inspiration a few times in my adulthood when I found myself stuck in a certain way of thinking or acting in work and in life.

Just play, I always remind myself. *There are no rules. Just play.*

> *"You might have to fight a battle more than once to win it."*
>
> **Margaret Thatcher**

During one of these unofficial practices, a car with a bunch of older kids in it pulled up alongside the field, making eye contact with me and holding it. Sure enough, they all piled out of the car and walked in my direction.

"Are you Bruce McCombs?" the biggest one in the bunch called out.

Uh oh.

I didn't have to be Einstein to figure out that there was going to be a fight, and that this fight wouldn't work out like the last one when my principal saved me. There were no adults within earshot, and I was on my own.

"I'm friends with John's older brother..." he started, and I just had to shake my head. John, again? That guy was becoming a real problem.

He continued, and I soon learned that his name was Luke, he was huge, and he was going to finish what John's older brother hadn't. Did I mention he was almost twice my size?

I am not going to survive this one, I thought, but then I quickly came up with a possible survival tactic just as old Luke was winding up to send me to the moon. Crouching, I ran at him with my lower center of gravity, picked him up off his feet, and slammed him to the ground. He almost landed on his neck! I held my breath until he moved a little, hoping that I didn't paralyze the guy.

No one uttered a word after that; Luke's older brother just picked him up and they left the practice field without even one backward glance.

When football season started, Coach Miller decided to elevate me from the eighth grade team to the ninth grade varsity. I felt so proud when I told my mother the head coach wanted me to move up, for no other reason than she knew the amount of time, energy, and passion I'd put into preparing for this moment during the hot summer months.

> *"The difference between ordinary and extraordinary is practice."*
>
> **Vladimir Horowitz**

Remember when I told you about Tommy? To refresh your memory, he was the star of our Halloween night match-up a few years back when I played for the Little Cowboys, and he played for the Jets. When we met again in junior high, Tommy blindsided me and hit me in the back.

"That wasn't a fair play," I told him.

He shrugged, and brushed me off. "Want to do something about it?"

I thought about his question for a minute, and decided his cheap shot was worth a fight. "Yeah," I nodded. "I'll meet you after practice and we'll settle it then."

Now, I was about the same size as Tommy, but he was mentally tough beyond his thin frame, and we had a pretty even match-up. After a few rough minutes of punching the heck out of each other, the coaches broke us up. I think they knew we had to get it out of our systems, and I also think they knew we had more in common than we believed. We were both workhorses and mentally tough, and we definitely both liked to win. Tommy and I became very good friends over the years, and shared many evenings playing poker together. I often thought of my brother during these card games, remembering how much he enjoyed poker and how much fun he and his friends had together.

> *"We do not remember days,*
> *we remember moments."*
>
> **Cesare Pavese**

My friends and I were mostly well-mannered, but there were exceptions. Our drafting instructor, Mr. Smith, had poor vision. Looking back, I can't understand how they allowed a guy like that to teach us about precise technical and geometrical drawings! It seemed like there were a lot of mishaps and misinformation related to his eyesight shortcomings, but the one I remember clear as day was when my new friend Rick raised his hand to ask a question with his middle finger extended. Mr. Smith called on him as the class erupted in laughter, but he had no idea what could have possibly prompted our belly laughs.

"What's so funny?" Mr. Smith asked, and we all went silent. No way would we ever dream of telling him about Rick's prank. Poor guy.

Speaking of poor guys...

In the ninth grade, I was practicing throwing the shot put for the city's track championships. It's a complicated event that involves holding a twelve-pound steel ball at the base of your fingers, placing it just so under your jaw and pressing it into your neck, starting at the back of the designated ring facing away from the throwing direction, then whipping your body around, catapulting the ball as far as you possibly can. Like I said: it's complicated.

That afternoon, I was focused on improving my distance and working on my form so intently that I didn't realize my friend who was also named Bruce, had meandered into my line of fire. The shot flew out of my hand exactly like it was supposed to, and I instantly felt like this was one of my better attempts...until it hit Bruce in his head.

If I wasn't so scared that I'd knocked his block off, I would've started laughing at the dumbfounded look on his face.

"What hit me?" he asked, looking all around in wonder. Then he saw the shot at his feet and burst out laughing, and we all knew he'd be okay.

There were bullies then just as there are today, and I observed people treating others poorly. I figured I was in a position to help in one way or another; if I could talk someone out of bad behavior, that was certainly my preference, but I also wasn't afraid to fight when words weren't enough.

One of the bullies in our school was a kid named Terry, who liked teasing my good friend Louis about his wardrobe. I guess teasing is an understatement; Terry's taunts were merciless, and they really made Louis feel badly about himself.

I started off nice with Terry. "Hey," I said in passing. "Leave Louis alone, why don't you?"

That didn't work, and the teasing escalated.

"Knock it off, Terry," I ramped up my tone and added a scowl.

Still, Terry persisted. And that was that. I told Terry I'd meet him at the 7-Eleven to settle the matter. Interestingly to me now, this 7-Eleven in Oak Cliff, adjacent to my junior high school, was the first one ever built. Now, there's one on practically every corner.

Everyone at school started talking about the fight, and showed up en masse to support me. There must've been at least fifty kids, ten deep, surrounding the two of us and egging on the fight. Terry took off his glasses and came at me with a flurry of aggressive fist punches and kicks, but I defended myself and won the fight decisively.

After Terry gave in, he nodded at me and promised, "I'll leave Louis alone." He kept true to his word, a quality that I've grown to appreciate in a person.

As I got older, my classmates grew taller, bigger, and sometimes faster, but I continued to gain confidence in myself. I wasn't concerned with measuring myself against others, but more intent on comparing myself to the person I was the day before. My mindset wouldn't settle for anything less than success.

Do you know what helped during times I grew weary of pushing myself? I'd remember my older brother's words whenever I was about to complain: *Suck it up*.

Yeah, that worked.

Chapter Five
High School Highs

The summer before my sophomore year, I met Julie. She was a year older than me, and became my first serious girlfriend. She was beautiful with a delightful personality, and she had a terrific mom who always seemed interested and involved in her daughter's life. We broke up once I entered high school, but Julie went on to become a Dallas Cowboy cheerleader, pose for Playboy Magazine, and move to LA to be a fitness coach to the stars.

What a start for my dating history!

When high school football season rolled around, I secretly hoped I'd be elevated once again, this time to the varsity team. The invitation didn't come, though, and I assumed there was just too big of a delta between juniors and seniors and me. I played the first five games with the tenth grade junior varsity team, feeling more than a little unimpressed with myself. My goal was varsity, and anything less didn't fuel the fire inside me.

Then, two varsity running backs got injured, and I was called up to fill their slots for the remaining five games of the season. I hesitate to tell you that I was pleased with this development, as it came as a result of someone else's misfortune...but to be perfectly honest, I was pleased!

One of the guys I replaced was Rudy. Now, some people might describe Rudy as one of the greatest motivators on the team. He wanted to win, and had no shortage of persuasive energy on the field and in the locker room. Others might describe Rudy as the most feared guy in school. Both assessments were correct. After high school, Rudy went to the University of Texas in Austin and played baseball, working his way up after graduation to professional ball. For many years, he was the batting instructor for the Texas Rangers, our hometown team, and was responsible for many of the Rangers improving their batting averages during their World Series' runs, two years in a row. I'd say his motivational talents eventually came in very handy, wouldn't you?

Still, he was one of the few on the varsity team who treated me with respect; my other new teammates treated me like an underclassman and hazed me to no end. I carried the seniors' helmets and shoulder pads up to the practice field, and I also was forced to wait until all the older guys finished their showers before I was allowed to take mine. And that was on a good day! Yes, there were many nights when I came home unshowered.

I proved myself in my first varsity game, making eight unassisted tackles on defense and offensively running for sixty yards. I remember a fullback on the other team everyone called Big John, aptly so as he stood six-foot-two and weighed well over 200 pounds. He averaged 125 yards rushing per game, but not this night. We lost that game, but held him to only fifty yards. I think even Big John was impressed. He went onto play for Texas A&M, and then for the New England Patriots in the NFL.

We moved to another apartment complex while I was in high school, and this one had a lot more room to give both me and Patricia the privacy we'd been craving. It also changed the friends who were close-by and within walking distance, and I started hanging out more with a guy named Chuck.

I'd known Chuck since elementary school, and I'd always envied the atmosphere at his house. First of all, it was huge with two stories, and it had a pool table in the front room. I didn't know you could put a pool table in the front room! I'm not sure if it was a result of having easy access to a pool table, but Chuck ended up excelling in sports that required good hand-eye coordination like pool, baseball, racquetball, and golf.

Chuck's parents, Charlie and Billie, were also pretty enviable. They had Chuck when they were young – late teens or early twenties – so they were very mellow parents and allowed Chuck to have us over to hang out on the weekends. Charlie was an insurance salesman, and Billie worked for Trammel Crow, a well-known Dallas real estate developer. Charlie enjoyed staying in shape and went to the YMCA to lift weights several days a week, and Billie was smart and attractive. I looked at their relationship, and wished my mom could enjoy the same sort of dynamic with someone. Even though I'd hate to share her, it would've been nice if she'd had a partner to ease the burden and share the seemingly endless responsibilities of single parenthood. However, Mom decided that she did not want to make another mistake and stopped seeing men.

Chuck's girlfriend at the time introduced me to her friend, Jane, and we started dating. Before we met, I guess Jane dated a guy called Harry. I didn't know Harry since he was a year older and attended another high school nearby, but I quickly learned that he was much taller than me, about twenty pounds heavier, with an older brother who never met a fight he didn't try to finish.

Ask me how I know this.

Harry and his friends hung out at the intersection of Hampton and Illinois on weekend nights, halfway between our high schools. You could find pretty much every teenager in Oak Cliff milling about that area on Friday and Saturday nights, which was great unless someone named Harry was trying to find you to fight. I was able to avoid him for the first few months Jane and I dated, but then came one hot and muggy summer night when we were all playing pool at Chuck's.

"Hey, Bruce!" someone called through the open windows. "Come on out! Harry's here and he's going to kick your –"

Uh oh.

I looked outside to see the infamous Harry and about 15 of his friends waiting for me in the street. Of course, I went out to meet them. Of course.

> *"In youth, we learn. In age, we understand."*
>
> **Marie von Ebner-Eschenbach**

After a few choice words back and forth, Harry and I started to tussle. Then, Chuck's dad stepped out onto the front steps and shot his gun into the air! Even now, I remember how we all jumped when that bullet cracked the night in half, and how strong his voice was when he calmly warned, "You boys better get out of here."

It was cooler than a Clint Eastwood movie.

Football remained my passion all through high school, but my junior year team lacked in talent. We lost more often than we won, and I was disappointed in myself because I thought I should have showed more leadership. In May of my junior year, I had a meeting with key people that would be on the varsity football team.

"If we want to be contenders this year, we've got to start preparing now," I suggested. "You know what we should do? We should practice two hours every day during the summer."

A few of them groaned, but we all knew I was speaking the truth. If we worked hard, we'd show up for the season in peak condition and hopefully have a head start on our rival teams. The only thing more excruciating than playing football in Texas during a September heat wave, is playing football in Texas during June, July, and August.

"Success is sweet, but the secret is sweat."

General Norman Schwarzkopf

I eventually persuaded most of the players, but it was a tough sell. Most of us worked during the summer, and also enjoyed an active dating and social life, and it was difficult to find those two-hour windows when we could all practice. But practice we did.

Our hard work paid off for our first game of the year. South Garland was a new school built in an upscale neighborhood in one of the Dallas suburbs. It was hot and muggy, and exactly the type of night we'd envisioned during the summer. We were as prepared as we could get.

I was co-captain, which meant we'd have to meet the opposing team's captains in the middle of the field for the pre-game coin toss. The ref would throw a coin in the air, and the visiting team had to call heads or tails before it hit the ground. The winner of the toss got to choose their starting position, either offense or defense. There are a lot of studies and statistics about that first choice in a game, and we generally always chose possession of the ball; the more a team has its hands on the ball, the more opportunities they have to score.

That night, I was a little surprised when I saw South Garland's captains. They looked like grown men on their way home from work with their five o'clock shadows and menacing stares! I went back to the sidelines a little shaken, but I didn't let on to my other teammates how imposing they seemed. I was captain, after all, and my job was to boost their confidence – not crush it.

We all played a sloppy game with both sides experiencing their share of mistakes and turnovers. But I ran for over a hundred yards and scored a touchdown to help us win 12-to-seven. Let's keep my two missed extra points to ourselves and focus on the positives, shall we? Afterwards, our coaches were impressed but cautiously optimistic. We didn't care; this was a big upset in Dallas-area high school football, and we were psyched to start our senior season with a win like this.

We lost our next two games by slim margins, which hurt but not as much as total routs would've crushed our unbridled optimism. Then came our battle with the Kimball Knights, one of our biggest crosstown rivals.

The Kimball campus was located adjacent to the very impressive and somewhat daunting Sprague sports complex, which was considered their home turf. That was our first obstacle. The second was that Kimball was heavily favored in the game. Their players were bigger and faster, and they had beaten two highly-ranked teams prior to our contest.

I watched Kimball films until my eyes glazed over, but all of a sudden something clicked. I'd been attending poker games with Bubba long enough to know how to spot a tell, and we'd found one! Before every offensive run, one of Kimball's running backs leaned in his stance a certain way. If he leaned left, it signaled a running play to the left. If he leaned right, it signaled the opposite. We also learned that if the runner was in his proper stance – straight up and down – that Kimball was going to execute a pass play. This intelligence allowed us to shut down their running game, and also allowed us to rush the passer with abandon because we knew when they were passing.

The Kimball game turned out to be my best games of the year, offensively and defensively. On offense, I gained almost a hundred yards and scored two touchdowns, including a 53-yard run, and I kicked a 40-yard field goal. Defensively, I made 13 tackles, helped jam the offensive line, and won the Dallas Morning News Defensive Player of the Week. We beat Kimball 33-to-three.

"Spectacular achievement is always preceded by unspectacular preparation."

Robert H. Schuller

The next team on our schedule was Pinkston, another new school that opened its doors in 1970. On April 20, 1971, the United States Supreme Court upheld the use of busing to achieve racial desegregation in schools. However, the residents that lived in the Pinkston area were primarily Black, so their high school reflected that area's population. Very little integration had taken place.

There was uncertainty to live in that period of history, and the many courts' challenges to the desegregation ruling. I'd overhear some older ones express their views, but all I could think was that I was happy to have had Bubba's influence in my life. He never judged someone for the color of their skin, or how much money they earned, or any other qualification a lot of adults used to determine whether someone was worth it or not.

I scored two touchdowns in the Pinkston game and kicked a 42-yard field goal into a stiff 25-mph wind, which happened to be my longest successful attempt, and we won the game 40-to-zero. There are many reasons why I'll never forget that game, especially for the longest field goal of my career.

It was also after that game when I learned that some teammates were taking uppers to boost their energy. Never one to be left behind when it came to improving my performance, I tried some of those pills in a subsequent game. They definitely gave me a pep in my step, but I hated the side-effects. My heart raced so fast, I thought I was having a heart attack. I decided I'd just stick to my usual routine of hard work and motivating thoughts to help me reach the next level.

My senior season ended spectacularly in a game against our crosstown rivals. It was a crisp, cool Friday night for football, and the stands were packed for both schools. Adamson was the oldest school in Dallas and their team included a few guys who I skirmished with years earlier. (Yes, most of those skirmishes began with those fateful words: "Are you Bruce McCombs?") Both teams came into the game with winning records, so this would be the game that determined Dallas' unofficial champion. I didn't even have to motivate the team that much in the locker room, as our collective tension and anticipation were at an all-time high.

Most athletes have that one game that stays at the forefront of their memories, and I am lucky enough to have made one of those forever souvenirs from the Adamson game.

As we walked from our locker room onto the field, the stadium lights pierced our eyes, blazing against the backdrop of the pitch black sky. I recall the unmistakable smell of fresh-cut grass, and the relentless attacks of the swath of bugs keeping watch over the game. Wayne, our quarterback, was especially sharp in the pre-game warm-up.

We drew first blood when a halfback pass landed in the end zone, which put us up seven-to-zero. Adamson came right back running off tackle, and scored on their first offensive possession. Their defense stopped our next possession on four downs. The opposition continued running successfully off tackle, and marched down the field. We stopped them on four downs at our one-yard line for a goal-line stand.

On our first offensive play, Wayne threw a nine-yard square-out to Charlie, one of our receivers. On the next play he handed the ball off to me. I hit the hole at the ten-yard line, cut left at the 40, broke two tackles, and then cut back to the middle of the field where another tackler dove for my feet. Not tonight, son. I high-stepped to avert that tackle, and went on to score a 90-yard touchdown. Too winded to kick the extra point, my backup placekicker sent the football through the uprights making the score 14-to-seven going into halftime.

After my long run, Adamson marched down field and tied the score at 14-all. They continued to run off tackle, and were successful because their tackles were slanting down on our linebackers – including me. I told Travis, our other linebacker, "I can't stop these guys!"

At halftime we made appropriate adjustments by moving me and Travis to down positions instead of standing erect, which essentially gave us a seven-man front. Then, Travis and I slanted in the opposite direction toward their offensive tackles while our defensive tackles rushed the offensive player in front of them. This halftime adjustment filled the hole where they were running, and the technique enabled us to shut their offense down. Wayne threw for over 200 yards, and we rushed for almost the same yardage, and I'm proud I carried a majority of the latter stats.

Although we weren't on our home field, our girls' performance team was there to form a victory tunnel. My girlfriend was on the The Bisonettes, and she congratulated me with a big smile and warm hug before we boarded the team bus for the short ride home. We had a few traditions after winning games – like the Bisonettes victory tunnel – and leaving on the bus interior lights was one of them. Cars honked as we passed, either in celebration or with a hint of bitterness, and none of us stayed in our seats that night.

If someone bottled that post-football victory feeling, I'd buy it by the caseload. Everyone would. We ended my senior year with a terrific winning season, and the first winning record in four years. It was one of the greatest times of my life.

A few weeks later, I attended my final football banquet. Our guest speaker was Leroy Jordan who played middle linebacker for the Dallas Cowboys, which was an impressive get; the Cowboys won the 1972 Superbowl against the Miami Dolphins a couple of months later. Unfortunately, I don't remember much about Leroy's speech, but I do recall receiving our team's All-Around Player award for the season. My final stats for the year were better than what I expected when the football season began; I ended up rushing for nearly 800 yards and scoring over 100 points. I kicked a record 42-yard field goal, and was named to the All-City Football team by my peers. But none of that was my proudest accomplishment.

It was Red, our head coach, telling those in attendance that night, "Having Bruce on the team was like having another coach on the field."

If this was what success felt like, sign me up for life.

Chapter Six
And Then There Were the Lows

It was time to think of life after high school, and I had some pretty good ideas about my next steps. They included, in no particular order, finishing my high school career academically strong, being awarded a football scholarship to The University of Texas or LSU in Baton Rouge, and absolutely no more fights. I also wouldn't mind drinking alcohol. See, our football team made the collective decision to play at the top of our abilities during the season, and hangovers sure weren't the way to make that happen. I was looking forward to letting loose just as soon as I secured a full-ride.

I spoke to several college recruiters who visited our school, and I thought I made a good impression with each of them. Surely, with my coaches' recommendations, my proven work ethic, and my final stats, I'd receive an offer. But I waited. And I waited. Then I went on invited tours of LSU and North Texas, enjoyed them immensely, and waited some more.

You can probably guess how this story ends, but I was crushed when I didn't receive any offers to continue my football career with a university program. The rejection rattled my confidence, shaking me straight back to my grandmother's disdainful "You're just like your father" and the feeling that I was born to be one thing and one thing only: not good enough..

My optimistic list of next steps shifted, too, as I crossed off every item on it. I no longer cared about school, the ship had sailed – or, rather, sunk – on a football scholarship, and I'd continue fighting for the foreseeable future. Only this time, I'd be fighting myself.

One more thing: I'd definitely be drinking.

My buddy Travis and I started hitting Luanne's, a local nightclub for teenagers. Before we'd pick up our dates, we'd slam a couple shots of bourbon to get in the mood for dancing. But that was only the beginning of The Drunken Adventures of Bruce and Travis. We once hopped in Travis' purple Volkswagen bug and drove to Wichita Falls to watch the state semifinals for high school football. Wichita Falls was a perennial football powerhouse in the 60s and 70s, and they were set to play our crosstown rivals, the Carter Cowboys, for the chance to be in the finals. We wouldn't have missed that match-up for anything.

We crammed a couple of other friends named Freddy and Adrian into the tiny backseat, throwing in a case of Schlitz Malt Liquor for the ride. Several miles outside Dallas and with most of the case depleted, we *had* to relieve ourselves, but there was no rest area to be found. So, we pulled that purple bug over, hopped out, and waded into the waist-high grass along the side of the interstate.

Suddenly, we saw headlights pull up behind Travis' car, the unmistakable bloop of the brief police siren, and two Texas State patrol officers got out and started walking toward us, flashlights beaming in their hands.

"What are you kids doing out there?" one asked.

"The car antenna blew off," I responded.

"Looking for snakes," one of the others said at the same time.

After a brief conversation, the officers nodded at us and sent us on our way.

"Make sure you throw the beer out of the car," they warned. "Be careful, and enjoy the game."

That was a close call, and should've scared me straight.

> *"There's no such thing as shoulda, coulda, or woulda. If you shoulda and coulda, you woulda done it."*
>
> **Pat Riley**

The hits kept coming. On another aimless night where trouble was my only direction, I was cruising Hampton Road, an always bustling street in Oak Cliff, in my mother's beautiful 1972 green Chevrolet Impala. Man, that was a gorgeous car.

Note that I say *was* because that is an important part of this story.

For no apparent reason, three dudes in another car shot us the finger and threw beer cans at my mom's car. *The audacity*, I thought, turning sharply into a Dairy Queen parking lot to follow them. Alas, I lost control of the car and slammed straight into a telephone pole.

Steve, The Dimensions' former bass player, was sitting shotgun at the time of the accident, with Freddie, Marcus, and Travis in the back. Marcus was the biggest in the car, tipping the scales at upwards of 250 pounds. On impact, the force of Marcus' body bent the front seat into a

V-shape, and Steve was propelled into the windshield, the glass shattering like a spider web. Thank God he got off with only a large knot in his forehead, and no other injuries.

When the first police car pulled up, I was shocked to see my good buddy Rick jump out of the back! He was riding along as a police intern, and used his relationship to convince the officer to let us go without ticketing me for reckless driving.

I deserved a ticket, though, and I knew it. Beyond almost killing my friends over a rude gesture by complete strangers, I'd disappointed my mother. Actually, disappointed isn't a big enough word for what I'd done; she was devastated. I knew how hard she worked to provide us with a nice life, and I also knew the blood, sweat, and tears that bought the Impala.

If you're keeping count, that's yet another close call that should've scared me straight.

Track kept me busy for a while, but I didn't have another sport to play when the season ended. Like the saying goes, "An idle mind is the Devil's playground," and boy did he play. Suddenly, I was in trouble more often than I wasn't, and anger was my predominant emotion at all times. Not receiving a football scholarship made me more than mad; it made me feel worth less than worthless. It absolutely crushed me.

I started dabbling in low behavior beyond the underage drinking, and smoked my first joint with Steve. The light-headedness, chattiness, hunger, and even the paranoia were all enjoyable – preferable, even – to the pessimism, panic, and despair I seemed to feel about my life and my future. It was an escape from reality, which I sought.

I was not a big fan of my reality.

Art and Marge were Steve's parents. Art worked in sales for AT&T, and Marge stayed home to take care of the family and household matters. At the time, I thought they were really fun and the complete opposite of my rather strict, overachieving mom. My mom worked hard and cared greatly about her legacy, while Steve's parents were much more carefree and lived in the moment. Most high-schoolers must gravitate a little toward their parents' polar opposites, especially during senior year when we craved more freedom and a lot less rules. In that respect, Art and Marge were perfect.

> *"We tend to learn from bad examples, but we should take care not to use bad examples as a rationalization of our own bad behavior."*
>
> **Cathy Burnham Martin**

Looking back, though, both of Steve's parents were open alcoholics; they didn't even try to hide it from others. They argued with a drink in one hand and a cigarette in the other, slurring their words and calling each other horrible, unforgivable names. *If that was what adult relationships are like*, I thought, *then I'm glad my parents divorced.*

We laughed at their behavior, but their addiction set a terrible example for Steve and his sister for the rest of their lives. Although it was nice to have a place to let loose, I was always so proud of my mom when I was there.

Steve's dad drove a white and gold Buick Riviera, and he'd occasionally allow Steve to take it out on the weekend. Intoxicated in some way or another, we'd all pile into the car and drive it across Beautiful Stevie golf course at speeds up to 70 mph. Steve would dodge sand traps and oaks, doing doughnuts, and we couldn't stop laughing. I don't know where our consciences were at that age; we didn't think anything of destroying the golf course many of us played on every day. I remember driving past groundskeepers repairing the fairways, feeling awful what had transpired the night before in Art's Riviera.

> *"All bad behavior is really a request for love, attention, or validation."*
>
> **Kimberly Giles**

Toward the end of the school year, Oscar and I went across the river – Trinity River, to be exact, which separates Oak Cliff from the rest of Dallas – to buy beer before school. Oak Cliff was a dry part of town, dating back to around 1956 when a group of Baptist ministers led a bitter fight to prohibit sale of alcoholic beverages in our town. They forged a campaign directed against a pack of sleazy bars, most of which fronted Davis Avenue, one of the main streets in Oak Cliff, and won 17,000 to 15,000. If we wanted to buy beer, we had to drive a couple of miles over the Trinity River to a liquor store who didn't care that we were underage.

Oscar and I bought a six-pack, drank it fairly quickly, then showed up at school around noon just in time for lunch. It was a new low for me to drink before school, and I knew it.

I took my tray, looked for an empty chair, and randomly sat down opposite one of the smartest kids in the school.

"Pass me the salt and pepper," I ordered gruffly.

I'm not sure if he sensed I wasn't myself, obviously inebriated and obnoxious, but he hesitated.

"Pass me the salt and pepper," I ordered again, this time louder and meaner, leaning toward him about three seconds away from punching him in the face.

"Stop picking on him!" one of the cheerleaders yelled.

"I'm not picking on the guy," I slurred my words. "I asked him for the salt and pepper, and he's ignoring me. But he's going to give me the salt and pepper."

"Leave him alone!" she screamed.

At this point, I think everyone in the cafeteria knew my outburst had nothing to do with salt or pepper. Within a few aggressive minutes, I was restrained by two coaches who escorted me to the principal's office.

In another part of the school, Oscar was fighting with the guy who used to date his girlfriend. He was also escorted to the principal's office. We both got suspended for three days, and they sent us home on the spot.

"You're a fool to keep dating that girl," I told Oscar as we walked out. "She's a real –"

Turns out, Oscar didn't appreciate me calling his girlfriend the B-word, and he promptly turned and hit me square in the face, knocking me to the ground. I tried to get to my feet, but Oscar warned me, "Stay down."

"When you don't face the consequences, there are consequences for that, too."

Frank Sonnenberg

Of course, I didn't listen. I was in the mood to fight the world that day. While I scrambled to regain my footing, Oscar kicked me in the face. I have never felt such pain or seen so much blood in my life, but by the time I came back to Earth, Oscar had driven away.

I was so upset when I got home – not because I'd been suspended from school, and not because I'd made a real ass of myself in front of my classmates, but because Oscar had beaten me in a fight. I called him right up and threatened him, more than a few times. His two older brothers finally told Oscar they were going to retaliate if I continued harassing him. I guess they were tired of taking my calls!

By the time we served our suspension, I'd cooled my temper toward Oscar, and he seemed to forget that I'd disrespected his girlfriend. But the anger inside of me still boiled, and I knew I was one accidental nudge in the school hallway away from another brawl. Despite the leadership abilities I'd worked hard to develop, despite the hard work I'd accomplished on and off the fields, it wasn't enough. It sure wasn't enough for a scholarship, and it wasn't even enough to get out of a school suspension. I was still, as my grandmother was fond of telling me, "...just like Bill McCombs." Heck, even Bill McCombs, the lowest human on the planet, didn't want any part of me. I would never be good enough. I knew it like I knew two plus two equals four.

When I returned to school, Ms. Woods, my English teacher, helped me shape a new attitude that improved my grades and made me a better citizen. She was extremely tough on me, but I was used to strong women in my life. In so many ways, she reminded me of my mother: strong, smart, articulate, and did not appreciate excuses at all. It was apparent that all she wanted from me was to work hard and take a few deep breaths before popping off with my temper. If I trusted and followed her process, she knew I could be the best student I could possibly be. With her patience and encouragement, she helped me earn a B in her class. But she didn't stop with English; she helped me excel in my other studies, enabling me to graduate in the top 25% of our class.

When graduation finally rolled around, I felt like I'd actually earned it. We held an after-party at the new Marriott Hotel in North Dallas. Bill, Chuck's younger brother, stood guard and watched over several kegs of beer we'd purchased earlier in the day and snuck up to the room.

A few of us went to the room early to make sure everything was in order, but Bill didn't answer when we knocked. Oh, and we knocked! We must've banged on the front door until our fists hurt, but Bill still didn't answer. Fearing the worst – not that something had happened to Bill, but that something had happened to our kegs! – we climbed up the trellis to get to the balcony. Luckily, Bill was a smoker, so he'd left the sliding glass door open. When we barged into the room, we were relieved to see that the kegs were safe, and that Bill was fast asleep. He *may* have taken advantage of the free kegs while he waited. We shook him awake, and prepped the room for the night's gala.

By ten o'clock, there was a crowd of guys celebrating our high school graduation and having a great time. The party ended around 5:00 am without incident. It's surprising that there were no fights or drama of any kind, but I think we were all aware that our time together had come to an end, and we were grateful for it. Twelve years of math and music, flashcards and football, study sessions and science experiments, getting it wrong and getting it right, and simply getting through it together.

It was good, but all good things must come to an end. Isn't that what they say?

They were right.

Chapter Seven
Growing Pains

The summer after my senior graduation started badly.

One night, my friend James picked me up to go drink beer in the St. Cecilia's parking lot. I want to think that we must have had plans after that, because it's embarrassing to think that cracking open a few cold ones in back of my elementary school was *the* destination for two cool graduates like me and James. But there we were.

Around 8:30 pm, a flashlight beamed through my window. My eyes adjusted, and I saw a policeman standing there, motioning to roll down the glass. He shone his light from our faces to the beers in our hands, and then the empty cans in the backseat, and made a decision.

"Pop open the trunk," he instructed James.

Wouldn't you know it, James had several tape decks in his trunk.

"You got receipts for these, son?" he asked, knowing the answer.

"No, sir," James stuttered. "I'm sorry, Officer, but I don't have any receipts. I...I threw them away."

"Well, where did you buy them?"

"I...well...I don't recall, Officer."

Well, that was enough for the officer to conclude that the tape decks were stolen, and he was correct in his assessment.

"Do you know anything about these tape decks?" he asked me.

"I know nothing about those tape decks," I replied, using what I thought was my most trusty tone.

It didn't work.

The officers asked us to get out of the car so they could handcuff us, which was one of the most unpleasant, degrading experiences of my life. They read us our rights, then asked if we fully understood those rights – we nodded, not fully comprehending what was happening – and then they drove us to the main police station in downtown Dallas.

Once we were searched, fingerprinted, and booked, they led us to the same holding cell. I'm not going to sugarcoat it or try to sound like I was feeling brave at that point, because I was definitely feeling the opposite; it was scary, and I wanted my mom.

James and I didn't say a word. We just sat there in silence, listening to the echoes of the other inmates yelling at each other down the hallway. One of the most vocal was named Mr. Washington, and he seemed to have been there for a while.

"What are you in here for?" he shouted to us.

James, ever the smart alec, didn't think before he answered, "Murder!"

Well, he may have forgotten we weren't in our high school locker room, and the same sense of humor that landed there fell *very* flat in jail.

Mr. Washington didn't appreciate James' joke, and promised us, "I'll get you smart asses when we get in the bullpen."

"James!" I punched him in his arm, I was so mad. "You shouldn't have said anything! We're going to get killed in here!"

Our time to leave the safety of our holding pen eventually came when the officers moved all the detainees to the bullpen while the cells were being cleaned. There, we came face-to-face with Mr. Washington.

"Which one of you is the smartass who said you we were in for murder?"

We both kept our mouths shut and our heads down, and Mr. Washington and his friends moved on to another inmate. Thankfully, before any fights broke out, the guards escorted us back to our cells.

For us to get out of jail, we each had to contact our parents. James could not reach his, but my mother was home and waiting by the phone. I highly doubt that "bailing my son out of jail" was on her BINGO card that night, but I knew I could depend on her to come when I needed her. That was a real gift.

My mother met us at the jail door at 3:30 in the morning, and I could tell she was really, really mad. Her teeth were clenched, and her eyes were so squinted they were almost closed, but she was able to convey her disgust for me just fine.

That car ride was interminable, and no one dared say one word all the way to James' house. I'm sure he thanked my mom meekly, but she wouldn't acknowledge it. As soon as the car door closed behind him, she started speaking in a raised voice.

"When are you going to grow up? You need to do better, Bruce! Do you want to end up in jail? It's time to get serious about your future and get a decent job!"

It's a horrible feeling when the person you respect most in the world has lost all respect for you. I was ashamed, once again, to be me.

A few days after my arrest, I got a draft notice in the mail. My birthday, December 25th, placed me at number six in the draft, which meant there existed a very high probability that I would soon be in the military. My stomach sank, as I realized my entire life was about to change dramatically.

I went to the Federal Building in downtown Dallas to undergo a prequalifying physical. I was a little nervous, but I knew this was inevitable. The physician checked my blood pressure, looked mildly concerned, and loosened the cuff.

"Son, why don't you go back out to the waiting area for a breather, and then come back in about five minutes." He used a calm voice to get my blood pressure down, but it was still high five minutes later when he checked again.

Ultimately, I was denied acceptance into the military because my blood pressure was dangerously high.

A few days later, I was at my GP's office to get another physical needed to attend college, and my blood pressure was completely normal!

"Wait a second," I said to him. "Are you sure it's normal?"

"It's normal," he assured me.

"But I failed my military physical a few days ago because my blood pressure was too high."

"That's understandable," he nodded. "The draft experience probably excited you and elevated your vital signs."

To be perfectly honest, I thought it was unfortunate that I failed my exam because I probably could have used more discipline at that time in my life.

Once the military was taken off my list of options, I decided to throw myself into community college. I signed up for the summer semester to get a head start, and thought I was well on my way to changing my ways. My good friend Eddy, a friend and teammate since elementary school, had the same idea. Together, I thought, we were unstoppable. Bruce 2.0, here I come.

> *"Growing up happens when you start having things you look back on and wish you could change."*
>
> **Cassandra Clare**

Well, folks. I'm sad to report that the only thing I learned that semester was that I much preferred staying up late at night, listening to music, playing cards, and drinking beer over college. My mom was – no surprise – extremely disappointed in me, once again.

"Bruce," she said. "This isn't working out. If you aren't going to school, it's time to get a job and another place to live. I can't keep bailing you out."

She was right, of course. I started looking for a job immediately, but I couldn't shake the feeling that I was looking for so much more.

In a major instance of serendipitous timing, the illustrious Bill McCombs decided that he wanted to be part of our lives. He called Mom at the bank where she worked, and asked if he could come over to visit with Patricia and me. She agreed, but she came home that day and warned us, "I trust that man about as far as I can throw him."

Patricia welcomed him immediately, as I assumed she would. After all, this was the same girl who belted out *All You Need is Love* on repeat from the minute the Beatles introduced that song. While Patricia eagerly asked question after question about Bill's life, I sat back and listened. I didn't want to show interest because I didn't want to seem disloyal to my mother.

He stayed for about an hour, and on his way out he asked me, "Want to come to work with me one of these weekends?"

I hesitated, and then told him I'd let him know. After thinking about it a lot and wavering in my decision, I finally said yes, but I invited Eddy to join us. There was no way I'd hang out with Bill McCombs on my own. I guess a lifetime of hearing from family members who despised the man had an effect on me.

Bill was a department store vacuum salesman, and so we met him at Sears to watch his demonstrations. He was an interesting guy, and he seemed eager to show me all the insider information about his line of work. He invited us to lunch, and told story after story about his side of the family who I never knew existed. I learned that his parents were deceased, and his sister's boys owned a popular car wash.

"Oh, and you have two half-brothers," he mentioned, flooring me completely.

Brothers? Even if they were half-brothers, they were still family, right? I wondered how many times this guy had been married, but I thought I'd better save that question for Patricia.

After lunch, Eddy and I thanked Bill for the interesting day, and I wished him well. I was keen to leave, but I also felt compelled to stay just a little longer. It was a strange, foreign feeling.

"When can I see you again, Bruce?" he surprised me by asking.

I didn't know what to say because I really wanted to discuss the day with my mom, so I answered, "Let me get back with you."

As soon as I got home, I told mom and Patricia about my visit with Bill. "...and we have two half-brothers!" I told Patricia, who squealed with delight. More family, more love was always her cup of tea.

"Well?" Mom asked. "Did you enjoy yourself?"

I couldn't be sure if she wanted me to say I hated it or if she wanted me to be happy that I'd finally met my father, or if she simply wanted me to come to my own conclusion. But I wanted her to know that my loyalty was to her, and that I appreciated how she'd devoted her life to giving me mine.

So I shrugged and said, "It was alright. We'll see."

Patricia, of course, couldn't wait to meet with Bill again. However, her joy was short-lived.

Like me, Patricia was going through her own growing pains. In fact, she'd moved out of the house at an early age because she felt like there was so much more life to live beyond my mom's rules. To my mom's dismay, Patricia dropped out of high school to work, and was living with an older guy named Larry.

When Bill found out, he told Patricia in no uncertain terms that she had to move out and stop living with Larry. She was understandably annoyed, and I understood her reaction completely. How dare he impose his fatherly input on our lives when he hadn't ever been our father?

> *"Parents can only give good advice or put them on the right paths, but the final forming of a person's character lies in their own hands."*
>
> **Anne Frank**

The conversation between him and Patricia got heated, and Patricia told him, "Where I live and with who I live is none of your business. You're not welcome around here anymore!"

Afterwards, Bill wrote my mother a letter. In it, he apologized for abandoning us, and told her how sorry he was for the way he treated her when they were together. It was a touching letter, but I did not appreciate the words at the time. I was still too young to forgive the pain.

The next time we saw Bill McCombs was at his own funeral.

At the time, he was living with his oldest son, Henry. One day, he was out riding his bicycle and just died of a heart attack. What a way to go.

We met Henry and Mike, our two brothers from another mother, at our father's funeral. Their features were strikingly similar to Bill's, but they were taller. As always, Patricia was curious and wanted to learn more about the other side of the family, so she chatted with the two brothers after the funeral was over. The three of them got busy and planned a trip to visit Henry in Del Rio, Texas along the Rio Grande River, where Henry lived. While there, Mike and Henry went bird hunting and Patricia hung out with Henry's wife. They all continued to hang out whenever their paths crossed, or they passed through Dallas.

I was happy that she'd finally gotten something positive out of her short encounter with Bill McCombs.

Chapter Eight
Onwards and Upwards

My mother's consistency as the hardest worker in any room paid off. She'd made her way up from her starting role as a bank teller to a loan officer, and eventually was promoted to Vice President, Small Business Loans. That's where she met many of her high-value customers, including the general manager of Allied Van Lines. Through her connections, I got a summer job there.

The job at Allied was hot, back-breaking work, moving furniture locally throughout the North Texas area. It was not unusual for the temperature in July and August to be over 100 degrees with 85% humidity. I made only $2.25 an hour, but it afforded me to pay my rent, put food on the table, play cards, and buy beer! What more could I want? I also learned how to drive a semi-truck, which gave me more responsibility and seniority than most of my co-workers. We moved furniture from 7:30 am until the job was done, which could be close to midnight. Of course, we earned overtime, too, but at $2.25 per hour that was next to nothing.

Every so often, I'd pick up a six-pack of beer and stop by Steve's little apartment. Steve worked as a respiratory therapist at St. Paul hospital, just down the street from where he lived. His place became a safe refuge for me to hang out. It made sense when he asked me to move in and help him pay rent, mostly because my mom was still after me to leave if I wasn't going to pursue college.

"Yeah," I told Steve. "That would be great. And, boy, will my mom be happy!"

I don't know if *great* truly encapsulated my new living arrangements. Steve's unit was no more than 350 square feet, with a tiny kitchen, tiny bathroom, and tiny shower. We rearranged it so we could fit two single mattresses, a coffee table, and two dining chairs in the main living area. No, it certainly wasn't great, and it wasn't even comfortable, but it wasn't a bad start for two guys fresh out of high school with no money. I was grateful, and I promised myself I'd use this place as a launching pad for a bigger and better life.

I found the long and unpredictable work hours didn't contribute to my usual routine of healthy breakfasts and dinners at a set time around my mother's table. I learned that if I wanted a snack, there wouldn't magically be one waiting for me like there'd been in my mother's icebox. At Steve's, there were only two things in the refrigerator: milk and beer. The milk was there only because Steve was a big coffee drinker, and enjoyed a splash of milk to soften the taste. I started buying groceries that could be prepared quickly, and paired well with water and/or Coors beer.

Now, I was 5'7" and normally clocked in at around 180 lbs. Within a few months of living in my own place, I gained 30 pounds, which put me around 55 pounds over my recommended weight. Drinking and eating with little or no exercise had my gut spilling over my belt, and my friends started calling me Goodyear Blimp! When we played cards, a few of the guys would ask, "Are you in, Blimp?" I laughed along with them because we'd all given each other pretty ruthless nicknames, but deep down it hurt.

I'd expected so much more for myself, and I was disappointed with the way I was turning out. I felt like an out-of-shape loser without even a *basic* plan for my life. I started doing drugs, which sent me into the next level of despair. If you knew me then, you'd wonder why I never wanted to be around my friends, why I was suddenly so lazy, and how I managed to hold a job when one simple task overwhelmed me.

> *"Don't wish it were easier.*
> *Wish you were better."*
>
> **Jim Rohn**

The only thing that saved me was having my mother's mantra drilled into my subconscious for my entire life: "Bruce, always remember to stay humble and outwork others." I was never late for work at Allied. Never.

Some of my friends were driving dump trucks for a construction company that hauled asphalt for road repair. The hourly rate was $10 and as much overtime as you could handle. I didn't have to be a mathematician to run the numbers; this job paid way more than my piddly $2.25 per hour gig.

As luck would have it, I got an interview right away and was hired on the spot. Fantastic news, right? Wrong. After only a few days – a few hours, if I'm being honest – I knew I'd made a mistake. Driving a dump truck for 12 hours every day in 100-degree heat was a real ball buster, and this assessment was coming from a guy who moved furniture up and down stairs for a living! To this day, I can't smell tar without shuddering.

I quit after one week, but I didn't feel badly about that; I decided to turn the crummy experience into something a little more positive.

"What did I learn from this?" I made myself answer this question truthfully. And the truth was that despite my behavior of late, I knew that I had more potential than this job could offer me. I knew I could earn a better living elsewhere.

One of my old football teammates was an ironworker, working 40 hours a week and making $15 an hour. I studied and passed the ironworker's certification test, and got started. Within just a few weeks, I was working on a ten-story office building. After welding on several construction sites at much higher elevations, I decided that I didn't particularly enjoy heights. Nine months after I started, I quit.

> *"Aim higher in case you fall short."*
>
> **Suzanne Collins**

I was unemployed for several weeks until a friend of mine told me about his job as a route salesman for Coca-Cola.

"The pay's good, and the benefits are better," he told me, so I applied immediately and got the job.

My duties included delivering Coke products to supermarkets and convenience stores, which doesn't sound like much, but it was respectable. It paid better than ironworking, didn't involve tar or heights, and it gave me confidence to know that my employer was Coke. I was proud for the first time since I graduated high school, and I really felt like I was advancing myself.

My supervisors noticed my performance, and continued to give me a larger territory and more prestigious accounts like Kroger and Safeway.

Every delivery driver has a story – that moment when your life flashes before your eyes, and you wonder how in the world you're going to make it, still employed – and I certainly have mine. It was a hot and humid Friday afternoon, and I'd just finished my last delivery of the day to a 7-Eleven. I was covered in sweat to the point where you could see the stains under my arms. I was completely depleted. I couldn't wait to get home, change out of my sopping wet uniform, and crack open a cold one. I drove a little quickly out of the parking lot and ran a curb, which caused my truck to tilt a bit to the right.

Well, bottles upon bottles of Coke tumbled out onto one of the busiest streets in Dallas because I'd forgotten to close the passenger bay door! Fortunately, we carried brooms and dust pans on the truck for emergencies like this, but it took me a while and traffic on both sides extended as far as you could see. One of the local radio stations was out reporting on traffic in their helicopter, alerting everyone to take a different route, if possible, because some Coca-Cola delivery driver had made a giant mess.

When I returned to the Coke distribution center, the news was all over the radio. After one look at my face, they knew that I was the driver who'd caused the traffic jam, and burst out laughing. I didn't feel too badly; they all regaled me with their own stories, and some were even a little worse than mine!

I worked at Coke for about a year before deciding that I wanted a less-strenuous job with more opportunity for career advancement. I'd improved from my Allied job, but I knew I was nowhere near my potential, and I wanted to earn a more substantial income.

My reasons weren't wholly professional. I'd started dating Jane, a younger girl from a well-to-do family. Her mother owned a training school for beauticians and barbers that she franchised throughout the state of Texas, and she had some misgivings about me from the start. Mainly, she didn't particularly like that I was four years older than her daughter and that I was unemployed. So we dated for four months until her mother persuaded her to stop seeing me.

When Jane was breaking up with me, all I could hear was my grandmother telling me, "You're just like your father." I felt inferior, second-rate, and shiftless. I'd seen my mother work three jobs just to scrape by, and I decided then and there that I was going to make so much money that no one would ever discount me again.

A few months after leaving Coke, I found a job delivering industrial shelving for W.W. Cannon. Their customers were primarily auto parts and industrial machinery companies. I was making more money, but I could also see avenues of potential advancement beyond just driving a truck.

Part of my responsibility included taking sales orders from the salesmen, and making sure the shipment was properly assembled in the warehouse. If the order was filled and delivered correctly, the salesmen praised me. If not, I and my supervisor would hear about it. Hence, I triple-checked to make sure that all deliveries had the correct bills of lading, and my reputation soared.

Eventually, I was promoted to the warehouse manager, and started working even more closely with our sales team. They'd walk into the warehouse like they owned the place, perfectly coiffed in their crisp white shirts and ties, checking on their orders and racking up the money.

I remember telling my friends, "The salesmen get a lot of respect. And I like the way they comport themselves. I want to do that. I know I'd be successful."

They really inspired me. I started eating a healthier diet, reducing my alcohol consumption, jogging, and lifting weights.

Steve and I were making enough money now to move from our efficiency into a two-bedroom apartment in an upscale part of Dallas. The apartments were newly-built and had lots of girls our age living there, too. It seems important to add that these girls loved to sunbathe by the pool every weekend. I needed to look good for them, as well as for my future job as W.W. Cannon salesman, so I started running on the tree-lined trails by our new place.

I was at a crossroads, and I knew it. I was still doing recreational drugs, but I certainly wasn't pushing the edge like some of my friends. It wasn't fun to watch, and it was even less fun to help them get high. David always asked me to inject him with diluted pink diet pills. He got them from a doctor who was writing prescriptions for just about anyone who walked into his office, and they were supposed to help with weight loss. I took them, but David *really* took them. First, he mashed up the little pink pills, then transferred that powder to a spoon and mixed it with a little bit of water. He heated the spoon from underneath, which turned the mixture into a syrup of sorts that could be drawn into a syringe.

David asked, "Will you help me inject it?"

I was hesitant and said, "What if something goes wrong?"

He noticed my nervousness, and said, "Just tie my arm with this large elastic rubber band to dilate my vein, and then I will inject the solution myself."

I watched his face turn beat red as the speed rushed through his body. Shortly after, David's pupils dilated, and he seemed agitated.

I told David, "You are on your own after this, buddy." It was awful.

"Drugs are a waste of time. They destroy your memory and your self-respect, and everything that goes along with your self-esteem."

Chuck Palahniuk

I didn't have a lot in common with the guys who experimented with needles. Maybe it's because I grew up with a strict mother who I'd never want to disappoint more than I had already, but I had standards for myself and injecting drugs into my bloodstream wasn't on that list. It feels like an excuse to tell you that everyone was doing drugs and pushing the limits, but that was the truth of those times.

It was time to decide who I wanted to be, and this wasn't it.

Chapter Nine
Laissez Les Bon Temps Rouler

It was the early 1970s. The Beatles had just broken up, and other bands began to flourish, like Led Zeppelin, Pink Floyd, The Eagles, The Who, and, of course, The Rolling Stones. When the bands toured and came through Dallas, our posse went to the concerts together.

We pre-gamed hard before the concerts, making sure we were lit just enough to really enjoy the vibes, smoking a little bit of weed and drinking a beer or two. Anything more would've interfered with actually experiencing the bands. The arena was always raucous, with beach balls flying everywhere until the emcee finally introduced the main event. And then, when the stadium lights dimmed, we all fired up our lighters and the smell of marijuana filled the air.

"I'm afraid concerts spoil people for everyday life."

L.M. Montgomery

One of my favorite concerts was held at the world-famous Cotton Bowl in July of 1975, on the State Fair of Texas campgrounds. It started at 11:00 am with bands I don't recall, and by 4:00 there were 50,000 fans sweating in the 100-degree weather, waiting for The Eagles and The Rolling Stones to take the stage. Girls were topless, and the guys ran naked while being sprayed with giant water hoses. We paid $20 each for great seats, a few rows back from the front of the stage. I'll never forget it.

The Eagles played first to get the crowd revved up, with tunes like *Peaceful Easy Feeling*, *Witchy Woman*, and *Desperado*. After they finished their set, Mick strutted on stage wearing an Uncle Sam outfit, and we went wild. Their first song was off their relatively new album, titled *It's Only Rock and Roll.* They played for over two-and-a-half hours, including their biggest hits: *Satisfaction*, *Get Off My Cloud*, and *Time Waits for No One*. I can't remember many $20 nights that brought me so many lasting memories, but this one definitely did.

A few weeks after the Stones concert, I was in an accident where I lost control of a motorcycle and slammed into a tree. Travis was in town and happened to be behind me on another bike. Since he was an experienced bike rider, I trusted him to lift the motorcycle off me to relieve the pressure. He then called 9-1-1.

As the paramedics loaded me into the ambulance, Travis sarcastically asked, "Did you take your eyes off the road, Jack?"

"That's *Hit the Road, Jack.*" I wanted to strangle him for joking in my time of need, but it hurt too much to move. Travis called all our friends to let them know I was in the hospital. When they stopped by, they asked, "How are you?" Not Travis. He asked, "How's the nurse?"

As soon as I healed up again, life was good.

One of the places we enjoyed socializing was the Travis Street Electric Company, a terrific spot to dance, meet girls, and play foosball. Marcus, a high school football teammate, worked his way up to become the assistant manager. He later opened a sister night club in Tyler, Texas called – you guessed it – the Tyler Street Electric Company. After one of our visits to see Marcus, we drove on to New Orleans to attend Mardi Gras. Freddy and Adrian joined me for the trip, the same characters who accompanied me and Travis to Wichita Falls to see a high school football game.

We had to sleep in the car the first night because New Orleans was at full capacity, but we found a place near Bourbon Street the next night. It was a dump, but it kept us dry.

Bourbon Street was the definition of wild, and we were shoulder-to-shoulder with thousands of other crazies, drinking Hurricanes and having a blast. It definitely felt claustrophobic, and I wished we'd been a bit better at planning spur-of-the-minute trips like this; the people who had the foresight to make reservations were all hanging off the balconies lining the street, throwing beads down on us. I had never seen so many people in one location in my life.

Bourbon Street has an interesting story. French engineer Adrien de Pauger designed the street layout of New Orleans in 1721, and chose one to carry the name of the French Royal Family ruling at the time: Rue Bourbon. It extends 13 blocks through the French Quarter, and has stood the test of time, remaining the center of Creole French and Spanish societies. Creoles of color developed the neighborhood as their social center, but when Americans moved in, it became known as the French Quarter.

> *"When a lot of people are calling it a night at 2:00 am, New Orleans is coming alive."*
>
> **Mannie Fresh**

Fat Tuesday, translated from the French Mardi Gras, represents the last night of eating rich, fatty foods and drinking copious amounts of alcohol before fasting 40 days during the Lenten season. Boy, did we follow the tradition! The festivities ended on Ash Wednesday when Lent begins, so we hopped in the car for the long nine-hour drive home, a little worse for wear.

Since New Orleans is a coastal city, fog is a big problem, particularly while driving at night on I-49 north. The fog was so thick that the visibility was less than 20 feet. Instead of driving 70 mph, I drove 50 the first couple of hours because it was so difficult to see. I finally asked Freddy to drive so I could take a nap. After fading off to sleep, I woke up to see Freddy passing a large semi, heading right toward an oncoming semi with headlights flashing.

"Freddy! What the %$#@ are you doing?!"

Freddy sped up and made it back into our lane, barely missing a head-on collision.

"We could've been killed!" I was incredulous. "Pull over. I'll drive the rest of the way."

I don't care how tired I was; I wouldn't have been able to sleep a wink with Freddy at the wheel!

> *"Friendship is the hardest thing in the world to explain. It's not something you learn in school. But if you haven't learned the meaning of friendship, you really haven't learned anything."*
>
> **Muhammad Ali**

I consider myself lucky to have had really meaningful friendships. Any time I wanted to do something or try something new, I had a buddy to accompany me. Now, this wasn't always a great thing; it would've been better if I had a friend who said no once in a while to some of my bad ideas!

But poker was always a good idea. I loved that game since the days of my youth when I'd accompany my brother to his meet-ups, and now I had friends of my own who played regularly.

Our group played all sorts of games that most people have never heard of, including 7/27, Push-Tittle, Dynamite (aka Guts), 4 by 4, and 5 by 5 (aka Iron Cross). We also played traditional games like Five- and Seven-Card Stud, Blackjack, and Texas Hold 'Em. The games were played at different venues, from our apartments to cheap motels and garages. There were three things I could count on during those poker nights: we'd drink a lot of beer, smoke a lot of weed, and we'd play until two or three in the morning.

Great times.

At the beginning, the maximum amount we played for was around $50. As we got older and made more money, the poker pot got larger, with Dynamite and 7/27 normally producing the largest payouts.

Our rules for Dynamite were pretty simple. We started with two or three cards, and the person with the highest cards – three Aces – won the hand. We also played low card Dynamite, with the one holding an Ace, two, or a three winning. If ever there were several players with competing hands who thought they had the best cards, they could elect to stay in the game...on one condition. If a card player stayed and *lost*, then they must match the pot. Therefore, say the pot was $100 and three people stayed to vie for the win, the two losers had to match the pot and pay $100 each upon their loss. The pot for the next hand would be $200 plus each person's ante, which was usually around $20. Thus, if there are five additional players, it would cost $300 to stay in the next game. For this reason, we liked at least seven people in play to maximize the winnings.

If my memory's correct, the largest pot we ever had was $3,300. My good friend was the unfortunate one who had to write an IOU to the winner. This matching concept definitely caused the game to get out of control for young guys with meager incomes, but there's just something about poker that kept us all coming back.

> *"Life is not always a matter of holding good cards, but sometimes, playing a poor hand well."*
>
> **Jack London**

I was an average card player who won just about as often as I lost. Poker is about taking risks, and I didn't take many because I didn't have discretionary income to just throw away. The beauty of poker, for me, was the chance for us to get together and talk about what was happening in our lives, network about better job opportunities, and razz the heck out of each other.

One of the best parts of poker nights, though, were our field trips to Jack-in-the-Box in the early hours of the next morning to buy their famous tacos with secret sauce. Some guys could eat ten tacos at a time, but I'm not naming names.

Chapter Ten
Out West, With a Bottle in My Hand

Life, up to this point, was mainly about me; a not-so-special series of events punctuated by my mom's – and my own – disappointment in me. One night, I was regaling my mother about my latest set of goals and aspirations, vowing that this time would be different.

"Bruce," she interrupted. "I have something to tell you."

You probably already know this, but my mother was one of the unselfish ones. Whatever I had to say, she'd be the first to listen with rapt attention for as long as I wanted to talk. She was a very private person who rarely spoke about herself. Whatever she was about to tell me was sure to be important.

"I've been diagnosed with Stage 1 Cervical Cancer," she stated matter-of-factly, without fluff or hesitation. "But my doctor says it hasn't spread to any other tissues or organs, so my prognosis is good."

Cancer. Just hearing that word felt like a kick in my gut.

> *"I think all of us are always five years old in the presence and absence of our parents."*
>
> **Sherman Alexie**

I don't remember a time growing up when my mother even felt sick. If she did, I certainly wasn't aware of her calling out of work or sleeping it off in bed. Honestly, I had never been so scared in my life.

"Don't worry," she assured me. "My cancer has a higher cure rate than other cancers. All I need to do is..."

She told me her treatment plan, which included a hysterectomy followed by a course of radiotherapy to help prevent the cancer coming back. She might have well been speaking Mandarin because I didn't understand a word of it. I just tried to focus on the "Don't worry" part.

But I worried. Boy, did I worry. And, for the first time since I'd stopped attending church and practicing Catholicism, I kneeled down and prayed.

"God," I begged. "Please cure my mother, and protect her entire being so the cancer will not spread."

Then I took it to another level, making a pact with God, Himself.

"If you cure my mother," I bargained. "I will change my behavior. I will become a better person who is more thoughtful and kinder. Just please cure my mother."

After mom's surgery and a few months of chemotherapy, we received the fantastic news that her cancer had not spread! It was in remission! Her doctor said that she would be monitored for a few years to make sure the cancer stayed away, and I am pleased to report the best spoiler in the history of spoilers: My mother's cancer never returned.

It was now time for me to hold up my end of the bargain with God, and I gratefully pivoted from who I'd been to who I'd become. A few of us are lucky enough to experience epiphanies in our life, and while I wish she'd never had to endure the pain and fear involved with her cancer, I was happy I'd gotten the chance to change.

My pact with God was the catalyst that helped me make my most important life decision to date: to finally earn my college education. I kept the decision to myself just in case I might change my mind, or on the off-chance I might fail, but I eventually confided in Steve.

"What?" He was genuinely confused. "But you're making so much money! We have a nice place to live! We have poker tonight!"

I had to laugh, but my decision was final. I made a commitment to change, and I was going to keep my word. From that day forward, I stopped smoking cigarettes and quit all forms of drugs, drinking alcohol, and – gulp – playing cards. I moved out from our bachelor pad, dropped 60 pounds, and lost my hot temper. To keep my expenses down, my mother allowed me to move back in with her, in her new luxury apartment, for the next couple of years.

I began my first semester at community college in the fall of 1976, starting with 12 semester hours of classes. Since I needed a job and enjoyed photography, I also got a job working for Fox Photo. We didn't have a steady stream of customers, so I was able to study when the store was empty. I was either studying or working, with a little sleep in between.

Like many students, I was uncertain about what I should do with my life. A counselor asked me what I enjoyed, and I thought about that question a lot when choosing my major, finally settling on biology and psychology. I wanted to know more about how humans worked and how we thought, and everything in between. Maybe because I enjoyed my courses, I studied harder and made excellent grades.

> *"Time and time again, we've seen that*
> *one person can make a difference.*
> *There is no reason why that person can't be you."*
>
> **Wayne Gerard Trotman**

A few weeks before my college summer session ended, a schoolmate told me that she had her palm read by a bohemian rhapsody. She wasn't talking about Freddie Mercury's song; she meant an artist who dealt in predictions and fantasy.

"I'm not kidding," Judy told me with wide eyes. "My reading showed me my life's possibilities! You've got to give it a go, Bruce. It will change your life."

I've been open to new things my whole life, so I followed Judy's advice.

The palm reader had a quirky house that smelled like a concert that never ended. Fishnets hung from random hooks, there wasn't a matching color or pattern anywhere, and black lights barely lit up the place. The walls were covered in tapestries, scarves, and oversized photos of John Lennon, Eric Clapton, and Mick Jagger.

Crystal matched her home if that makes sense. In her early 40s, with sooty lashes and dark hair cascading just as casually as her long skirt and bare feet, she smiled like she'd been expecting me. And what a smile she had.

She knew nothing about me – this was in the time before internet! – and she gazed at my palm to find clues about my future. There were a few observations she made, all very accurate and pretty astounding, but one thing she said really intrigued me.

"Your destiny lies in the West, with a bottle in your hand."

"Like a wine bottle?" I wrinkled my forehead. "I doubt that's accurate. When I was younger, I drank cheap wine and got really sick. I've hated wine ever since."

Crystal smiled at me and shook her head. "I cannot see what the significance of the image of the bottle is, but it comes into your life."

What a waste of fifty bucks.

A few days later, I told my mom that I'd been thinking of taking a trip to San Francisco.

"It's a great music scene," I said, telling her about Janis Joplin, The Grateful Dead, and Jefferson Starship.

"One of my customers – Larry – now lives in San Francisco," she replied, telling me that Larry was originally from Wills Point, Texas which is about 30 miles east of Dallas. "I'll ask him if he can show you around the city."

She called him, and he assured her that he would be happy to give me a tour and a place to crash when I came into town. This would be my first solo trip, and only my second trip out of Texas, so I was grateful for the help.

Off I went, west to California.

Hey. Maybe Crystal was right.

Larry lived in two-bedroom house atop Twin Peaks, a famous landmark named for a pair of 900-foot high summits looking down on the city of San Francisco. It was exactly as you'd imagine a San Francisco neighborhood might look, with modern homes densely packed on steep lots along winding streets. There was usually a thick marine layer hazing up the scene, especially during the summer when the fog rolled across the Golden Gate Bridge. As we toured the house and he gave me the lay of the land, Larry told me that he had to travel to LA for a few days, so I would be on my own until he returned.

He suggested that I check out the classic San Francisco landmarks including Alcatraz, Fisherman's Warf, Napa Valley, and Lombard Street, the famously steep, one-block section of San Fran with eight – EIGHT! – hairpin turns.

"When I get back, I'll take you across the Bay to Sausalito," he promised. "On a clear day, we'll be able to see San Francisco's downtown skyline. It's beautiful."

I couldn't wait to see Alcatraz, a small island of only 22 acres that was discovered by Spanish settlers who named it after all the pelicans – or alcatraces – nesting there: Isla de los Alcatraces. It was sold in 1849 to the United States, who promptly built the first lighthouse on California's coast on the land. Other buildings followed, including military fortification and a military prison, until it became the most famous federal prison we know from the movies and lore. All the worst criminals were housed there, including Al Capone, George "Machine Gun" Kelly, and the Birdman of Alcatraz.

It wasn't impossible to escape from Alcatraz, but it was pretty darn hard; the water currents around the island were always high, which greatly decreased the chance of an escape. Alcatraz closed in 1963 mostly due to the difficulty of transporting fresh water to the prison and removing waste away from the island. But there was also the morning of June 12, 1962, when a guard making a routine headcount came upon three inmates apparently still sleeping in their bunks. No matter how hard he banged on the cell bars, they wouldn't rouse. Why? Turned out, the inmates in question were actually dummies, their heads made from painted paper with real hair glued to them. The prisoners – the armed robber Frank Morris and the bank-robbing brothers Clarence and John Anglin – were gone. Vanished in the dark of night. The guard raised the alarm, and the warden promptly notified state and federal authorities. An intensive manhunt began, but the three were never found.

My tour was so interesting. I learned that it was also too expensive to run Alcatraz, costing nearly $10 per prisoner per day, as opposed to $3 at other prisons. Over half-a-century of saltwater saturation had severely eroded the buildings, and it would've taken too much money and manpower to rebuild. But the worst story I heard that day was that Alcatraz prisoners who were put in solitary confinement found themselves in a pitch black cell, and their toilet was a hole in the concrete floor. I understand they broke the law, but that seemed a little inhumane to me.

Upon my return from Alcatraz, I walked through Fisherman's Warf to hail a taxi and checked out places to eat. I couldn't be there and not order fish, so I grabbed a shrimp plate at one of the takeout restaurants. I'm not kidding; my tastebuds still remember the freshness of that shrimp!

Larry's house was amazing, especially at night. There was nothing better after a long day of touring a city than coming back, chilling on his patio, looking out at the San Francisco skyline from the top of Twin Peaks.

After a fabulous night's sleep, I was back on the streets of San Francisco. My first stop was Coit Tower, set atop Telegraph Hill, probably is the best location to observe a 360-degree view of the city. The tower paid tribute to all the firefighters who served the city, and was built from donations left by Lilly Coit's estate. She was an eccentric from the late 1800s who chased fires in her youth, and was known to smoke cigars and wear men's trousers. I think I would've liked knowing her, especially after learning that she was an avid gambler who never met a card game she didn't like. She quickly figured out that men accepted her in their games more easily if she dressed like a man. Smart.

I was able to walk Lombard Street, famous for supposedly being the most crooked street in the world. Built in 1922 at the request of Carl Henry, a nearby homeowner, as a remedy for the steep topography to their house, there are eight hairpin turns that cover 600 feet with a legal speed limit of five miles per hour. Since the incline grade was 27 percent, it was too steep for most vehicles, so creating the zigzag pattern was pretty brilliant. I'm not alone in that assessment; over 17,000 visitors a day during summer weekends agree, making it a top tourist spot in the city.

From there, I walked to the Golden Gate Bridge. What a memorable stroll! Partway across, the fog came rolling in and the only thing I could see were car headlights. San Francisco fog is a main character in the story of the city, and today Karl the Fog even has his own Twitter account with hundreds of thousands of followers.

Even though I was dead sure that I didn't like wine, I *had* to tour Napa Valley. At the time, it was the up-and-coming wine region in California. Italian settlers in the 1800s farmed the area, and many grew grapes until prohibition passed in the early 1900s and the vineyards were replaced by other legal crops.

> *"Americans drink wine just like we use to drink water before prohibition."*
>
> **Ring Landner Jr.**

My tour included stops at a few wineries, including Robert Mondavi. The Mondavi family came from Italy and settled in Lodi, California in the 1930s. They farmed vineyards after prohibition, making primarily jug wines. It wasn't until the late 1960s that Robert Mondavi became the outspoken cellar master, declaring that American wines could be just as good as French wines. He figured that one way to prove his claim was to have new and modern facilities built in Napa in the mid 1970s to showcase their work product. I was excited to see the place.

As I approached the entrance, I remembered the palm reading from Crystal I'd experienced just a few months prior.

"My destiny lies in the West, with a bottle in hand." I mumbled to myself. "This is way too coincidental that I've ended up here."

From the very entrance, the Mondavi winery countered every preconceived notion I had about vineyards. I'd assumed they were stuffy and judgmental, places where only those with discretionary income felt comfortable. Boy, was I wrong. From the minute I entered Mondavi, I could feel Mr. Mondavi's intention of wanting every visitor to feel welcome, as if they were an unofficial member of his family.

I learned so much that day. Our tour guide started by telling a baker's dozen of us what we could expect to see over the next hour. He told us about the relationship between soil, weather, and climate – or *terroir*. We also learned how human intervention and technology affect the outcomes, the importance of grape types, the different type of trellis or vines, pruning, and the harvest.

Then we moved from the vineyards to inside the winery where the grapes are pressed, and the wine is stored. Mondavi had its red wines aged in French Oak, and its white wines primarily stored in large stainless-steel tanks. Except for the reserve wines, the Cabernets were aged for at least one year before they were bottled for still another year of aging. The whites were aged for three months before being transferred to a bottle.

And here I thought it was a simple process, like that famous episode of I Love Lucy stomping grapes.

> *"Beer is made by men, wine by God."*
>
> **Martin Luther**

The tour guide invited us to the tasting room where we could sip a few varietals for free, but I was understandably cautious because of my first and only experience with wine. I ultimately tried it, reminding myself that this stuff wasn't cheap Boone's Farm! I learned that my favorite was cabernet because it was thick and robust, had a little grip (tannins), yet the texture was somehow smooth. We also tasted merlot, pinot noir, and a couple of white wines. It was all outstanding, and I quickly forgot that I hate wine.

When I stood beneath the arched entrance and looked west, I could see To Kalon Vineyard, named for the Greek phrase meaning *highest beauty* or *highest good* and where Mondavi Cabernet Reserve grapes are grown. Behind it were the western hills of Oakville that blocked the ocean's fog from reaching Napa Valley. It was breathtaking.

Our second stop was Freemark Abbey, another landmark winery that shaped viticulture in Napa Valley, and whose roots trace back to 1886. It was originally called Tychson Winery after its founder, Josephine Marlin Tychson, who happened to be the second woman to build a winery in Napa. In 1892, she suffered a loss of over ten percent of her grapes because of a parasite called phylloxera, and sold it to Anton Forni the next year. He renamed the vineyard Lombarda after the region of Italy where he was born, but the widow Tychson remained close-by in a large Victorian house overlooking her former farm. After she died, Lombarda sold to Charles Freeman, Mark Foster, and Abbey Ahern, who named it once again: Freemark Abbey. Their portfolio of wines included red and white varietals which tasted terrific to this neophyte wine taster.

Larry had returned from his trip by the time I made it back, and I told him all about my Napa experience during a wonderful dinner at Scoma's Fish House in Sausalito. Scoma's is a spacious waterfront restaurant serving seafood pulled straight off the boat with great views of the San Francisco skyline on a clear night. We also caught up on my tour of Alcatraz. Surprisingly, Larry had never been to the island, but I must've put a lot of energy and salesmanship in my description because he immediately added it to his bucket list of attractions to visit. Over the next couple of days, I introduced Larry to Mondavi and Freemark Abbey wines, we went to a hilarious comedic play, and hung out on Fisherman's Warf to people watch and eat.

The next morning, I packed my bags for the trip home, thanked Larry for his generous hospitality, and told him I'd repay his kindness if he ever found himself in Dallas. We probably couldn't compete in the fresh fish department, but Texas barbecue would do just fine!

It was a life-changing visit.

I can't help but think that Crystal had been very, very right.

Chapter Eleven
A New Start

I guess I've always looked at life as a series of adventures – some bad, some good, and others that belonged in a book – and I was ready for yet another one. Patricia and I had earned enough college credits and excellent GPAs that enabled us to be accepted at the University of Texas in Austin. UT was in our blood, as our mother is a Longhorn alum.

I had a customer named Ben when I worked at Fox Photo, and we developed a great relationship over time. He was a dentist who wanted to reduce his tax burden by investing in a Swensen's franchise. He'd seen my work ethic and offered me an assistant manager position. Like I've said, I was always open to new ideas, and this one could make me some money. Although I'd never managed people, I felt confident that I could motivate them and manage a business like I did at W.W. Cannon.

Training was on-the-job and came at me fast, which made the experience a little helter skelter at first. Teenagers were often unpredictable employees and didn't always show up when they were scheduled. Worse, they delivered poor customer service, and some were downright thieves. About three weeks into the job, the manager quit without giving prior notice. As a result, I had to work double shifts until Ben could fill the manager slot. I made great money compared to my prior jobs, but it was commensurate with the added responsibility and brutal hours.

Ben knew that I was headed to UT after the summer, but asked if I wanted to manage the business after his *second* manager quit shortly after *he* was hired.

"Sorry Ben," I told him. "I have only one goal and that's getting a college education."

My sister and I enrolled at the University in September of 1978. We both worked while attending school in order to pay for our education and living expenses. The only financial support we received was a monthly stipend of $100 from Mom to help pay for rent, and money from our Pell Grants intended to help students whose parents earned below a certain income threshold.

Fortunately, there was a Swensen's franchise in Austin right across the street from the campus. I walked in, spoke with the manager, and told her about my experience at the Dallas location.

"That's great!" she seemed happy to see me. "We happen to be looking for a manager right now! Would you be interested?"

Although I needed the money, college was my priority. I told her that, unfortunately, I didn't have the time to devote to a management position, but that I would work 35 hours a week. I started the very next day.

On my first day at Swensen's, I met all the employees and they welcomed me with open arms. I managed the counter in the afternoon, and felt like a bartender. Instead of mixing drinks, though, I was scooping ice cream and making shakes.

I signed up for 12 course hours my first semester. I assumed it would be easy since I'd carried a similar load at community college. Boy, was I in for a rude awakening. The coursework at UT was five times more difficult, and I quickly saw my grades plummet from As to Bs and Cs. My work schedule didn't help, and I was struggling to find the time after work to study for exams and complete assignments. It didn't feel like there were enough hours in the day to study after I got home from work, and forget about social clubs or a personal life!

I became really anti-social as my study hours became more precious. In fact, I don't recall going to even one football game, which was very unusual since I loved the sport and particularly UT football. I remember my mom taking me to the 1963 Cotton Bowl that pitted UT against Navy. We sat on the 40-yard line, about twenty rows up. Navy was ranked number one in the country, and UT was number two. Roger Staubach was the quarterback for the Midshipmen, and won the Heisman Trophy as a *junior*. Texas ended up winning that game handily 28-to-seven, and won the National Championship.

Looking back, I can't believe I missed out socially, but I was on a mission: study hard, finish school in a timely manner, and get a well-paying job.

My only mode of transportation was my blue Trek ten-speed and the campus bus. I rode my bike everywhere – in the heat, cold, rain, early in the morning, and late at night – which kept me in great shape and allowed me to enjoy the great outdoors. The only time I didn't enjoy riding was when it rained, and the moisture on the back tire flew up and splattered mud spots on my wet suit. I eventually put a guard on the wheel to prevent the debris from hitting me.

Moving on from Swenson's, I landed a cashier's position at HEB, a large supermarket chain based in San Antonio. I improved my pay once again, but I was working fewer hours than usual, clocking only 30 hours a week. HEB management liked my performance and my past experience managing many people, and asked if I wanted to take over the graveyard shift. My new position included supervising around 40 stock replenishment clerks and inventory checkers, and I enjoyed the quiet of the night work. But although the pay was fantastic, I got really tired of riding my bike late at night and then to school the next morning. After about six months, I was able to change back to the day shift working as a manager.

Along the way, I befriended a few customers that would regularly pass through my station. There was Mrs. Connolly and her six-year-old son Scott who were always good for a laugh. One day, she commented that she'd had just about enough of her kid's honesty.

I looked at Scott and asked, "So how are you doing today?"

His reply?

"My mother is fat!"

I was so embarrassed for Mrs. Connolly, and couldn't make direct eye contact with her as I continued to check out her groceries. But Scott's comment did not faze Ms. Connolly in the least.

She told Scott, "If you eat properly, maybe you won't be fat like me."

I'd come home with stories that had my sister rolling on the floor with laughter!

Patricia was working, too, around 30-plus hours a week bartending at small nightclub on Seventh Street. She earned enough to pay her expenses, and the hours were perfect.

One summer night, Patricia arrived home around 2:00 in the morning. I was up late studying, but had just walked into the kitchen to get a snack from the icebox. Suddenly, the room filled with red and blue flashing lights, and I heard people shouting in the front yard. I looked out the window to see two officers helping Patricia into the back of their car.

I ran outside to find out what had happened, and one of the officers told me, "Your sister was driving erratically, and we suspect that she was drinking while driving."

Oh, no. "Can you please remove the handcuffs?" I begged.

"Go back in the house," they shook their heads. "You can pick up your sister in the morning at the main police station."

She was booked for a DUI, and spent the night in jail. I wasn't able to bail her out until six the next morning. I'm not so sure she knew how lucky she was to have me picking her up rather than our mother, but I did my best to be supportive; I knew what it felt like to spend a night in lock-up.

Listen. I drank too much, too. I remember one afternoon, a few buddies and I took THC and added beer to the mix. A few more friends dropped by on their motorcycles, and joined in the debauchery. We took turns driving those bikes up and down the street, competing with each other to see who could rev our engines the loudest, making complete fools of ourselves in front of the neighbors. When we got back to the house, we turned on Pink Floyd's Meddle album full blast and listened to *One of These Days*, an extremely long, hypnotic track with David Gilmore playing terrific guitar riffs. After a few more beers, we all passed out on the waterbed.

"That's the problem with drinking, I thought, as I poured myself a drink. If something bad happens you drink in an attempt to forget; if something good happens you drink in order to celebrate; and if nothing happens you drink to make something happen."

Charles Bukowski

We were so out of it that we didn't notice that Doug passed out on the bed with a cigarette in his mouth. You can probably guess what happened next, and you'd be right. The cig fell out of his mouth and onto the bedspread, which quickly caught fire. I woke up from my slumber, smelled smoke, and yelled, "Fire! Fire!" The flames were about a half-foot high and covered a quarter of the bed before we were able to put it out. Our excesses almost killed us that day, and jeopardized others.

I have always wondered if my – and Patricia's – desire to drink was related to my father's alcoholism. Mom told me about their first years of marriage when he drank and mistreated her, but she really didn't go into much detail; it made her uncomfortable and brought back too many bad memories.

That DUI was an awful experience that changed Patricia's life for the better. Much like when I arrived at my own epiphany when my mom told me she had cancer, Patricia had her own epiphany when she got arrested. That was the last time she took a drink of alcohol.

She started attending AA meetings, met her first sponsor, and learned about working the steps whenever she had the urge to drink alcohol. She found a new job in the University's communications department, focused more on her health and studies, and her grades improved.

Another by-product of her sobriety was that Patricia's cooking became...ahem...inventive. After taking a macrobiotic cooking class to learn how food could cleanse her mind and body, she started making Sunday stew. Now, that would've been a great development if the stew included some meat, potatoes, carrots, and onions. But Patricia's stew was entirely seaweed, intended to flush her system of impurities. After weeks of bugging me to try some, I eventually forced myself to eat a little to placate her.

"Delicious," I lied, trying not to gag.

At her core, my sister was a rescuer. She was also an animal lover, and had a dog and two cats. Scruffy, who was a small Irish terrier, was hit by a car and crushed both hind legs, but Patricia didn't want that to stop her from getting around on her own. So what did she do? She had a special carriage built for her, of course. It's exactly what you'd expect from the *All You Need is Love* girl, right?

During my senior year of college, I was constantly battling whether I wanted to finish; working full time and maintaining a full class schedule was wearing me down. My coursework was tough. In my market research class, for example, our primary project was to help a real estate developer perform a market area analysis to determine the economic feasibility for a condo development. The project lasted the entire semester and required the same amount of time I was spending on the rest of my coursework. To make matters more difficult, I was picked as the captain of our research team, responsible for meeting with the professor and developer, and providing them updates and reports on our findings. (Don't get me wrong; I was very proud of myself, too. But, still exhausted.)

> *"College is like a fountain of knowledge and the students are there to drink."*
>
> **Chuck Palahniuk**

After the team gathered and analyzed the data, my job was to develop the presentation and present the results to the team members. Our outcomes suggested the developer would realize an estimated return on his investment in 13 months, and his profit would be $5.2 million. Moreover, he would have to convince Austin City Council that the fertilizer for landscaping would not harm a nearby creek. At the time, the

Austin City Council was concerned about commercial building and the effects it had on the environment.

We earned an A for our work, and UT got $5000 from the developer for our research.

We also had to present our findings to our entire class. There were four other teams that were tasked with different projects, and our team received the highest scores: 95/100 for the presentation and a 97/100 for the casework. I was never good with numbers, but I saw the power of analyzing data on the condo project and decided to focus on marketing as my major.

UT had its perks, and one of them was the access to great companies seeking graduates from our school to work for them. During recruitment, I interviewed with several including United Technologies' Magnet/Wire and Insulation division. I met with the Director of Training, Emma, for an hour. She found my work experience and academic background interesting enough to invite me to visit their campus in Ft. Wayne, Indiana.

My schedule was to meet with their Senior Vice President of Sales and the Vice President of Manufacturing, and tour their facilities. I found the campus old but clean, and it had a certain Midwestern charm. While we toured, Emma described their magnet wire and insulation products made from copper wiring, explaining its many uses, from air-conditioners to airplanes. After the plant tour, Emma coached me how to interview with the executives.

When I sat down with the SVP of Sales, one thing stood out about our conversation. He said, "You can make a lot of money in sales if you are persistent and sell value." At the time, I didn't know the significance behind his comment, but I soon would.

On my flight home, I kept thinking about getting that job offer, reminiscing about my time at W.W. Canon and how impressed I was with their salesmen. *If I get this job*, I thought, *I'll be well on my way to join that club.*

Boy, I really liked the sound of that.

Emma contacted me a few days later and extended me a job offer, rattling off the details. All I remember from that conversation was that there would be a June start date, and a beginning salary of $14,500. That was more money than I had ever earned!

I called my mother to get her advice, and she told me, "If you like the people and it makes you happy, take the job."

That was all I needed to hear. I called Emma and accepted the offer.

Even though I was wavering whether to finish my senior year, I told my inner saboteur that I was going to walk across the stage and accept the diploma that I had earned. Finding a job right out of college was proof that my hard work paid off. I had followed my mom's advice, and had stayed humble and outworked others – even when I wasn't the smartest person in the room!

> *"If you're the smartest person in the room, then you're in the wrong room."*
>
> **Richard P. Feynman**

On my very last day of school, I did what I had done for the past three years; I got on the bus to the intramural field to pick up my bike. When I got there, my bike lock had been spliced in two and was lying on the ground, and my bike was gone. I was angry for maybe a second or two, and then I had to laugh. If I had to get my only mode of transportation stolen, there couldn't have been a better time for it to happen. I was still going places...I just no longer needed my bike to get there.

Over the next several days, Patricia and I packed up our belongings and prepared for our graduation. Our mother drove down to attend the ceremonies, and we invited some friends, too: Louis, my buddy since childhood, and two of Patricia's closest childhood confidants, Diana and Janis. When the time came, we dressed in our black robes and caps, placing the tassels on the right side of the cap to signify that we had not yet received our diplomas.

Patricia's graduation was held at the School of Communication an hour before mine. Walter Cronkite graduated from the very same school in 1933, and it also counts Pulitzer Prize, Oscar, and Emmy winners among their alumni. I kept a picture of Patricia from that day, a huge grin across her face as she received her diploma from the dean of the journalism school.

Our guests then rushed over to Erwin Center – the basketball facility which seats 17,000 – to see me graduate from the School of Business. We needed the space because there were so many of us graduating. I also got a picture of me accepting my diploma from the dean of the business school with a grin so big I could have lit up the entire city of Austin.

Graduating was the pinnacle of my short life. I think about what I overcame to reach that point – a graduate of The University of Texas at Austin, School of Business –and I feel humbled and grateful. Patricia and I completed our education!

Or so we thought.

Chapter Twelve
Fort Wayne

After graduation, Patricia and I resigned from our college jobs, tied up all of our loose ends, packed up our stuff, rented a U-Haul, and moved back to Dallas. What a fun break that was, reconnecting with high school friends I hadn't seen since college and enjoying that college graduate life. I'd accomplished something really difficult, and this brief period at home was my reward. I slept in, golfed the afternoons away, went to dinner with friends, and met new friends.

I met one of those new friends while out with my good friend Rick at a hip restaurant off Greenville. There were a couple of young ladies seated at the table next to us, and we struck up a conversation that lasted a couple of hours. I talked to Debbie the most, and when she mentioned that she played tennis, that's all I needed to hear.

"We should play sometime," I suggested.

"I'd love that," she smiled back. "But I'm warning you; I've only played a few times."

A few days later, I called her to arrange a tennis date.

When I got to her apartment, we talked a little and then hit the courts. I started off easy since she'd told me she was a beginner at the sport, so imagine my surprise when her forehand flew back over the net like a rocket. She was good! I shouldn't have been shocked; Debbie played the forward position on her soccer team, which meant she was an offensive player tasked with attacking the goal. I soon learned that she was the fastest girl on the soccer team and the leading scorer, which impressed me to no end. But I really liked knowing she was a team player who got along with everyone she met.

> *"How beautiful it is to find someone*
> *who asks for nothing but your company."*
>
> **Brigitte Nicole**

We threw a party together so all of our friends could meet each other, and there was a moment during the night when I looked around and thought, *A guy could get used to this.* She was going to make it very difficult to leave Dallas for Fort Wayne.

I was definitely conflicted. I did not want to cut short this budding relationship, but I was also incredibly excited about my new sales career, going through the training, and earning $14,500 a year.

My family took me to the airport, and Debbie met us there. They'd met once before, and there seemed to be a natural connection between them – especially between Patricia and Debbie. It was hard not to think I was walking away from a really good thing. I got emotional as the plane taxied from the gate, tears filling my eyes as I waved to everyone from my window seat. I wouldn't see them for at least a year.

My new boss Emma was there to greet me when I landed in Fort Wayne. She drove me to the company apartment so I could drop off my belongings and freshen up. We then went to dinner, and she gave me an overview of what to expect during the next six months of training. She also recommended several apartments that offered short-term leases.

The next day, I met my new colleagues in the training program. They were much younger, more rambunctious, and probably academically smarter than me. One of the trainees had graduated from Notre Dame, located in South Bend, Indiana, about three hours northwest of Fort Wayne. My grandmother, a devout Catholic, was an avid Notre Dame football fan. She didn't care about any other sports, but she loved the Fighting Irish and wouldn't miss one of their Saturday games. One of the happy memories I have of her is watching her yell at the television if a referee made a call against her team, if her players fumbled a play, or – loudest yet – if they won.

The other trainees were from Florida, Miami, Michigan, North Carolina, and UCLA. It didn't matter that I had graduated from the University of Texas, which was a highly regarded school; I still had my grandmother's admonishment ringing in my ears. I wasn't good enough, and I'd probably never be good enough.

I was intimidated by their brash confidence at first, especially when I realized that I was the only one who didn't belong to a fraternity during college. I could tell they still liked to go out, drink beer, and burn the candle at both ends. In no time, I realized that they weren't better than me at all; they were just new at all this, way too cocky, making a little money, and feeling bulletproof. I'd done all that in the four years following high school, getting that experimentation, inflated overconfidence, and skewed priorities out of my system.

Heck, I'd burned the candle until it was a puddle of wax!

By the second weekend, I had a better sense of my peers and my bosses. The rumor going around was that my supervisor, Emma, got a little too close with some of her trainees. Worse, she repaid them with special treatment, better pay, and more lucrative territories once they graduated from training.

> *"I have great faith in fools –*
> *self-confidence my friends will call it."*
>
> **Edgar Allan Poe**

At this point in my life, I'd learned a few things. One of them was that rumors like this one spread like wildfire, and it was only a matter of time until her superiors learned of her proclivities. I figured I'd lay low until then, and hope my work ethic alone would merit those choice territories. I was cordial with her, but I never let down my guard around her or put myself in a situation she could misconstrue. This was my first experience with navigating company politics, and I'm really happy I rose to the challenge and found my way.

I rented a place just two miles from United Technologies' main campus, which was really convenient. I could've ridden a bike to and from work, or even walked, but I didn't have to do either; they'd given us company cars during our training period, which was one more excellent perk.

For several months I learned the properties and manufacturing processes of magnet wire and insulation. To this day, I can rattle off its many uses – they're needed to build transformers, motors, and generators, and even electric guitars – but it hasn't come up at a dinner party yet!

The training program was difficult, made even more so by the state of my brain. See, I'd starved myself to lose those 60 pounds, but what I didn't realize was that my brain lost neural function, too. Restricted eating like I'd embraced really affected my brain chemistry, which led to an inability to concentrate and memory issues. I didn't know any of this until I watched back my sales training videos. In them, I appeared nervous, tripped over words, and seemed genuinely confused.

The written exams highlighted my problem even more, as I had to reread each question multiple times before I understood its meaning. I'd lost all reading comprehension! My brain fog slowed down my response time, and I didn't get the chance to answer all of the questions. So, my test scores were among the lowest in my training class. Add that to my inability to string words together, and I was a sorry mess when it came to public speaking.

> *"Life is ten percent what you experience and ninety percent how you respond to it."*
>
> **Dorothy M. Neddermeyer**

When it came time for me to present on how magnet wire is manufactured, I was understandably anxious. If you'd asked me immediately afterwards how I did, I'd tell you I failed miserably. Somehow, my lack of confidence wasn't apparent to anyone else, and the tape recording showed a confident salesman well versed in all things magnet wire! In fact, I received the second highest score from my teammates and Emma.

As for my personal life, Debbie and I still stayed in touch, but I didn't really trust my feelings for her. We hadn't gotten to know each other that well before I left town, which made me cautious. I was lonely and far away from everything and everyone I knew, and I reminded myself to be careful not to get too attached. I sensed the same hesitation from her, as well.

But then there was my sister. Ahh, Patricia. She'd always dreamed of traveling the US, and she impulsively bought a camper to do just that. Her first stop was the famed tourist destination of Fort Wayne, Indiana to see her little brother.

When I saw Patricia pull up, all I thought about was climbing in the passenger seat and traveling back to Dallas with her. I had been with United Technologies for five months, and I still felt like I didn't fit. My younger cohorts didn't seem to have a care in the world, and I couldn't envision my future alongside them.

Rumors continued to swirl about my immediate supervisor, and I was nervous all the time that any interaction with her would end poorly for my reputation. Enough people were talking about Emma's purported misconduct, with rampant speculation that her job was in jeopardy. I spoke to her one day about securing a sales territory in Texas since she was the one who assigned them, and her response was tepid, at best.

"I can't really guarantee anything," she shrugged.

It was too much uncertainty for me.

And so, as I helped Patricia unpack her car and we chatted about her trip, I suddenly had a moment of clarity and blurted out, "I want to quit the training program and drive back to Dallas with you."

"Why?" she asked, visibly shocked. "I thought you were doing so well!"

I explained it all, realizing as I repeated my thoughts and concerns out loud to someone who genuinely wanted the best for me, that it all made perfect sense. This wasn't the place for me, no matter how well I was doing. This wasn't my future.

A week later, I resigned. When I told Emma, she stuttered and stammered like she couldn't find the right words.

"Why?" she asked with wide eyes.

I didn't tell her the truth. Instead, I gave her a vague reason like, "I need to return to Dallas to take care of some...family matters."

Fortunately, Emma did not dig further. She briefed her boss, and they both wished me well. Since I wasn't exactly leaving a job, there was no need for a two-week notice. I said goodbye to my teammates, and left.

It was the funniest thing. As soon as I left campus, I felt the sense of doom that had been following me completely dissipate. No more weight on my shoulders, no more waiting for the other shoe to drop, no more uneasy feeling in the pit of my stomach. I had made the right choice. I was dead sure of it.

The other thing of which I was dead sure? I was unemployed with no prospects in sight.

Chapter Thirteen
Onwards and Upwards

On our way back to Dallas, Patricia and I drove through beautiful Brown County, Indiana, over rolling hills with lush landscapes, and camped at Three Rivers in Kentucky. That lake was absolutely one of the most beautiful places I had ever seen, maybe because it reminded me of the Colorado River that streamed through Austin, Texas. Both were operated by a River Authority and Corps of Engineers, and used primarily for generating hydropower power for their surrounding areas, allocating water/irrigation rights, as well as recreation. After cooking a nice breakfast on an open fire, we packed up the camper and drove through Arkansas into Dallas.

> *"Humans, not places, make memories."*
>
> **Ama Ata Aidoo**

I think I'll count that drive back as one of my favorite life memories.

I made plans to stay with my mom until I could find a job. After three weeks of searching, I spotted a marketing analyst position in the Dallas Morning News' classified section at a company called Computer Language Research/Fast-Tax. I simply called the company, spoke to the receptionist, got the name of the decision maker, and sent my cover letter and resume to a woman named Wendy who was the Vice President of Marketing.

Although the job description preferred someone with at least two years of experience, Wendy agreed to an interview. I told her and the marketing team about the marketing research project I led while I was at the University of Texas for the real estate developer. When I got to the part about how we determined that the developer's return on investment would be over five million dollars, their eyes popped out of their heads.

That story plus my persistence did the trick, and I was offered the job. The starting pay was $19,500, a monumental increase from my short-lived job at United Technologies. I even had my own office! It didn't matter to me that it was the size of a refrigerator; I was just thrilled to have a space of my own.

There was a moment when I shook my head, incredulous at what I'd just accomplished: I was officially a marketing analyst for a high-tech startup. I knew that United Technologies wasn't the right fit for me, but who knew I'd land an even better job? I guess it pays to listen to your gut.

My new company processed financial data for accounting firms, corporations, and the financial industry. We were nearing an Initial Public Offering (IPO), and one of the key metrics to valuing the organization was its market potential and market share. In preparation, the CEO had Jim, his Chief of Staff, request that our marketing department focus all of our efforts on this task immediately.

Instead of speaking to my manager first, Jim came barreling into my office like a bull in a china shop, demanding that I clear my docket entirely and get started on the project yesterday. I didn't know how to handle him, but one thought popped into my head: Napoleon complex. If you're not familiar with this personality, thank your lucky stars. Basically, those individuals who are physically smaller and/or shorter than their peers sometimes develop an overly aggressive and domineering attitude to compensate for their...errr...shortcomings. No offense intended, but I feared that Jim was a classic case.

Bad luck for him, and worse luck for me.

Still, I was excited to participate in such important, meaningful research. My assignment required pulling data from various sources and inputting it into a new software program called VisiCalc. Over the Christmas holidays, I worked from 6:00 am until midnight learning the new spreadsheet while inputting data. Then on New Year's Day, Jim requested my presence in the office to explain my findings regarding the market potential of the company.

"I realize it's a holiday, but this is time sensitive," Jim told me.

Of course, I couldn't say no, but I wanted to strangle him. The demands he was making on my time didn't feel reasonable or fair, but I didn't know what to do about it. I was new, and that's the price a new employee pays at first until he or she proves themselves, right?

Wrong.

Luckily for me, I had one of the most skillful, most prescient business professionals: my mother. For heaven's sake, she was the first female Vice President at the largest bank in Dallas! I would be crazy if I didn't seek her advice on this matter at work.

"I think I'm being taken advantage of by Jim," I told her. "And I don't know what to do about it." I thought it might be too late to change our dynamic, but my mom disagreed.

"My bank has offered a lot of continuing education courses and trainings to help us develop into better leaders and communicators," she told me. "And I think that's exactly what you need. Find out how you want to communicate in business, and your interactions with Jim and everyone else at your company will improve."

I trusted her implicitly. Off I went to the freezing-cold library to check out books on winning communication styles in business. I learned there are four ways to communicate in business: passively, passive-aggressively, aggressively, and assertively. I fit neatly in the passive communicator description because, from the get-go, I hadn't expressed to Jim any of my wishes or needs. I realized that when he barged into my office that first day and demanded that I drop everything to help him, I should've said, "Can you please run this by my manager to make sure I'm clear to work on your project?"

After more study, I understood that my goal was to be an assertive communicator who expressed himself effectively and stood up for my point-of-view. It sounded wonderful in theory, but how was I supposed to put it into practice without alienating my superiors and especially Jim?

I didn't have to wait long. A few days later, Jim barged into my office once again.

"I need you to build a custom sales tracking system to track sales performance and commissions," he barked.

I understood the need immediately, since there were no customer relationship management solutions on the market the time. But I wasn't about to continue with a passive work persona – those days were over – and calmly asked, "Have you spoken with my manager?"

He looked at me sharply, more than a little surprised by my answer and my outwardly confident demeanor. It was a ruse; I was shaking like a leaf inside.

"No," he blustered. "I get my marching orders from the CEO, who both your manager and I work for!"

I nodded and repeated, "You will need to speak with my manager first, and then I'll be happy to take on the project once I get the go-ahead."

My heart pounded so loudly that I thought he could hear it from across the room, and fears of being fired on the spot raced through my mind. Jim's face turned beet red as he turned on his heel and stormed out my office, slamming the door and knocking my only picture off the wall. It was of The Three Stooges, who reminded me how much I loved to laugh and not to take myself too seriously.

"Why I oughta..."

Moe Howard,
The Three Stooges

I found the Vice President of Marketing a few minutes later.

"I was thinking..." I told her. "Since I don't know systems architecture and programming, would I be able to recruit a few colleagues who have those skills?"

"Great idea!" she said.

Both of the individuals I approached were honored I asked, and said they would be happy to help as long as their departments received equal credit for the project.

That was easy, I thought. *Now for the hard part.*

The next morning, I met with Jim. I had my pitch planned, and practiced it a few times to make sure I told him *what* I wanted and communicated *how* I wanted: assertively.

"Jim," I said. "I've spoken to the VP of Marketing, and think the project will go smoother if I add two colleagues to the group."

Jim wasn't having it because two extra people were not part of Jim's plan. "No. No one else. It will take too long if more people are involved."

I described the skills my partners had, and informed him that we felt confident we could have the system live in ten months.

Jim was quiet for a moment, clearly stunned, and then he said, "Wow. I was expecting at least a year. Set up a meeting."

It worked! And what's more, my team got the new system in place, live for the sales organization to use, in a little over ten months. With just a few tweaks, it worked correctly the first time upon company-wide launch.

I was proud of my work – on the project and on myself. I saw the connection between standing up for my point of view and advancing my career, and I was hooked. By asserting myself with Jim and asking him to go through the proper channels of speaking to my manager directly, I gained his professional respect. He never bullied me again.

> *"The measure of intelligence is*
> *the ability to change."*
>
> **Albert Einstein**

John, the Vice President of Sales, noticed the way I handled the project and the politics associated with it.

"Would you like to join my sales organization and make some real money?" he asked.

There was no other answer to that question than "Yes!" I'd been hoping to become a salesman ever since my first job at Allied. Before I knew it, I took over a sales position covering the Western US while based in the Dallas Metroplex.

My first sales calls were in Seattle, Washington, and the beautiful Puget Sound area. It was only a four-hour flight from Dallas, but it felt like another world. John took me to a seafood restaurant called McCormick's & Sons, which was within walking distance from our hotel. As we looked out at the ships circling and the seagulls swooping, I thought I was living in a postcard. It was *that* stunning.

John asked, "How do you like being in sales so far?"

I said, "I can't imagine it getting any better that this."

But it did. It certainly did.

The next day we attended meetings with executives who were responsible for operations in three bank trust departments. John led the meeting while I listened and learned how to conduct a sales call. John always asked questions that started with who, what, where, or how, a genius tactic to elicit a more detailed, engaged response than a simple yes or no answer. He also showed me how to qualify the prospect by finding out if they have the need, the money, and authority to buy our solutions. John didn't believe in wasting anyone's time if they weren't the decision makers. And, at the end of most interactions, John asked, "What's the next step?" It was an easy, active segue into sending over a contract or scheduling another meeting.

I learned more about the company I worked for during those tag-alongs with John. Computer Language Research, also known as Fast-Tax, was a service bureau that outsourced processing of tax information for the financial industry. It was a very big deal, and I can't believe my path led me to it. I got in on the ground floor of this high-tech organization before it hit the IPO market. How exciting is that?

Over the next several months, John helped me learn our technology and showed me how to present the features and the benefits of our solutions. His mentorship served as an excellent launching pad for me to excel in sales.

But the moments I remember most clearly are the ones when I made silly mistakes.

> *"Being positive doesn't mean ignoring the negative. Being positive means overcoming the negative. There's a big difference between the two."*
>
> **Marc Chernoff**

John and I once met with a man named George Dombrowski, the Senior Vice President for a large money center bank in Kansas City. He was a big deal, for sure. George told us that he played golf the day before, regaling us with stories about his favorite courses and clubs.

"Looks like you got a sunburn," I noted, pointing at his forehead.

His eyes widened as though he was shocked by what I'd said. "No, that's a birthmark."

If I told you I almost packed it up and left my job for good that day, I wouldn't be exaggerating. John glared at me, and I wisely kept quiet for the rest of the sales meeting after apologizing at least three times. Afterwards, he offered me a few pointers, one of which was, "Don't ask personal questions when you're not sure of the answer!"

A few days later, John and I met with Mr. Luciano, an Executive Vice President at one of the largest banks in the country. He was tall with striking gray hair, talked with a New York accent, and was very fit. John took the lead because he feared I might say something out of pocket, and I was happy to take a back seat. Oddly, Mr. Luciano refused to make eye contact with me throughout the entire meeting.

It was so obvious of a slight that I became fidgety and extremely self-conscious. What had I done? Was my boss aware that this was happening? Did I have something in my teeth? Should I jump into the conversation? All of these thoughts swirled through my mind, but I didn't do anything; I just sat there and waited for it to be over.

At the end of the meeting, Mr. Luciano shook my manager's hand and completely avoided shaking mine. Now, *this* was odd! *Extremely* odd!

"I'll be right back," I told John after we'd left his office, heading to the restroom. I took off my coat, looked in the mirror at my tie and shirt, and went to unzip my pants...which were already unzipped! My fly had been open for the entire meeting!

I didn't say a word to John when I rejoined him at the elevator bay.

"Did it feel tense in there, or was that just my imagination?" he pondered.

"I didn't notice a thing," I shrugged, hoping for a quick and painless end to the conversation.

After only a few sales calls with him, taking notes on his method, I started making my own calls. Not all of them were raging successes.

My first time out by myself, I met with the Vice President of a large money center bank in Phoenix. I kept telling her about how our solution could help her maintain headcount while adding more business, despite the fact that she kept telling me that she was not interested.

Finally, she stood up, leaned forward, slapped her hands flat on the desk, and shouted, "I AM NOT INTERESTED."

My jaw dropped as she pulled her hands back, audibly scraping the wood with her fingernails. It sounded like nails on a blackboard.

Was it something I'd said?

I apologized profusely for my behavior as I picked up my jaw from the ground, packed up my belongings, and exited with my tail between my legs. Doggone it. I'd forgotten one of John's biggest lessons: stop talking and listen.

As soon as I got back to Dallas, I sent her a card to apologize again. She eventually softened after I invited her to a Jimmy Buffet concert, and I was able to build a great relationship with her, making one of the largest sales in the company's history.

After a few minor hiccups, I earned three times more in my first year in sales compared to my prior role as a product manager. I honed my sales skills, which included developing a model to calculate our customers ROI if they used our solution, and it enabled me to climb up the leader board to earn top sales leader in the financial sector for two consecutive years in a row, and the accompanying prosperity continued to rise.

My territory gave me ample opportunity to travel beyond my sales calls. While in Phoenix for that disastrous meeting, I stayed over the weekend and visited Sedona, just a short drive north. I loved the red rock topography and its proximity to the Grand Canyon. I've also always loved a good western, and I knew many had been shot in that area including one of my favorites: *Broken Arrow* starring Jimmy Stewart.

I had to gasp when I turned left off Interstate 17 onto Highway 179. I clicked off the radio, sat in complete silence, and felt overwhelmed with emotion at the unbelievable beauty of the burnt red landscape and the rocks' geometric formations. The town center was at the intersection of 89A and 179, and I found the perfect place to take in all my senses a few blocks down atop a rock formation close to Airport Lookout. From this perch, I had a breathtaking 360-degree view of Sedona.

I sat there for a couple of hours, listening to someone in the distance play a Native American song softly on their tom-tom drum. I'd started reading about healing energies and spiritual reverence in some personal growth books, and I can tell you they were telling the truth! It moved me tremendously, and I kept visiting that spot every time I found myself in the area.

Pretty soon, everyone wanted their own piece of this magical land. Traffic and tourists took over, replacing the pure and mystical energy with high-priced developments for the highest bidders. It was no longer the place where I could recharge myself and refill my positive energy tank, but that was okay by me; I appreciated what it had given me for a few years, and would always be enchanted by my memories.

Debbie and I eventually got married, but the travel with my new sales job was hard on our relationship. I was gone several days of the week and that took a toll on us. I guess our downfall came from my absences, although she joined me on extended travel added on to my business trips. Perhaps the example Debbie's mother set having gone through multiple divorces influenced her decisions. All I know is that we didn't add enough to each other's lives, and made the decision to move on. She went to work for Tony Robbins, the famous life coach, and really turned her life into something about which she could feel proud; I don't think she ever felt meritorious during our marriage.

As for me, I got busy and decided this was a time to learn new things, like how to play the classical guitar. I also took cooking and social dancing lessons, and, of course, learned more about wine. I wanted to be more well-rounded person, for myself and for whoever I might meet along the way. I was not alone, as I dated women in my half-hearted attempt to find a life partner while still battling feelings of not being good enough. But yet, I was still pretty lonely.

I doubted I'd ever find my perfect match, my one true love. That kind of thing only happened in the movies, didn't it?

Chapter Fourteen
Heroes

After my divorce, I moved back to my old stomping grounds: Kessler Park. Nostalgia aside, it was such a convenient area, two miles away from downtown Dallas, and close to both airports, cool restaurants, and leisure.

I was making money, had old and new friends, and a busy schedule full of work. When I had free time, I was usually playing my guitar, having friends over for wine and dinner, sharing new dishes I learned in my cooking classes, and trying out my new social dancing moves. I really enjoyed country western dancing and west coast swing!

My mother saw a listing for a condo in the area, and I scheduled a viewing of the property with the owner, who was married to Nancy Lieberman, a terrific basketball player and coach when she was in her prime. I could definitely see myself living there, and then Martina Navratilova pulled into the garage as we were leaving. Turns out, she owned the condo along with Nancy when they were living together, and subsequently sold the property to Nancy and her husband. That *really* sealed the deal. We chatted for a bit about how she loved the area and was sad to leave, and I told her I grew up nearby and loved the area, too. Nancy was a fair and straight-forward negotiator, and soon enough I was the proud owner of a condo once owned by one of the greatest tennis players who ever lived. It was a neat brush with fame.

Back in my old stomping grounds, I fell into old patterns and started running again. My trail was the nearby golf course on Kessler Parkway until it dead-ended, and then I returned using the same jogging path. The roundtrip was about two miles, and meandered through custom homes, surrounded by huge oak trees, sloping hills, and a small stream called Coombs Creek. It was the calmest part of my day. Running got me naturally high, cleared my head of any negative thoughts or worries, and allowed me to check on my mother whose place was not far by foot.

But you probably know by now that I was competitive. Soon, I was competing in 10K races, and my best mile pace was just under six minutes.

I entered the annual Turkey Trot for the first time, a course roughly eight miles long, with a range of around 7,000 participants from serious runners to local celebrities and parents with babies in strollers. This particular Thanksgiving Day was crisp and cold, about 28 degrees, with no wind and no clouds in the sky – the perfect day for running. The route started in Downtown Dallas, crossed the Commerce Street bridge into Oak Cliff around Lake Cliff, and then back to Downtown for the finish.

> *"The reason we race isn't so much to beat each other...but to be with each other."*
>
> **Christopher McDougall**

The crowd dissipated after a while, separating itself into all the different paces. I happened to glance over to the left, and almost tripped over my feet; Roger Staubach was running alongside me! The former Heisman Trophy winner in 1963, and the two-time Super Bowl winner and quarterback of the Dallas Cowboys.

You already know he was one of my longtime heroes from back in the day when my mom took us to the Cotton Bowl in 1964. He was quarterback for Navy playing against my mom's – and eventually mine, too – alma mater. After that game, Roger was drafted by the Cowboys in the tenth round, number 122 overall. I continued to follow Staubach's respectable service career when he became a lieutenant, served in Vietnam, and exited the Navy in 1969, four years after the Cowboys drafted him. He ended up playing for the team for 11 seasons, the entirety of his field career.

I became a devoted Cowboys fan, largely because of Roger Staubach. Don Meredith, aka Dandy Don, led the 1966 team to the division championship game against the dreaded Green Bay Packers. For the next 20 years, the Cowboys enjoyed a winning season under the direction of Tom Landry and Tex Schram, the head coach and General Manager, respectively. At first, Tom was known as the coach who couldn't win The Big One, after consecutive losses to the Packers in 1966 and 1967 in that infamous Ice Bowl, which was one of the coldest games on record at 13 degrees below zero. I don't know how our players did it. Then, the Cowboys lost to the Baltimore Colts in the 1971 Super Bowl.

But Staubach helped change this streak when he joined Dallas in 1969, leading his team to the Super Bowl five times – four as the starting quarterback. With him at the helm, the Cowboys won Super Bowl VI and Super Bowl XII. Notably, he earned the Most Valuable Player at Super Bowl VI, which made him the first of four players to win both the

Heisman Trophy and Super Bowl MVP. He was nominated for the Pro Bowl six times during his NFL career.

The Cowboys' winning ways, flashy uniforms, and consistently high TV ratings endeared them to fans across America and all over the world. Thus, the Cowboys have become known as America's Team, and Roger Staubach's nickname was Captain America. He is regarded as the most popular player in Cowboy history.

And in case I haven't made this clear, Roger is regarded as one of the greatest quarterbacks of all time.

Back to the Turkey Trot. It meant the world to me to see Roger running the race beside me. Growing up, I didn't have a father figure, but I had Roger Staubach on my television every weekend. I saw him, Tom Landry, and Jack Nicklaus as men with impeccable reputations who held the admiration and respect from most people around the world. I'm pretty sure no one ever dismissed them and their contributions, and I looked up to them. They were the fathers I never had.

> *"Someone once said that every man is trying to live up to his father's expectations or make up for their father's mistakes."*
>
> **Barack Obama**

Sometimes, when my grandmother disparaged me with, "You're just like your father," I wished my father had been one of those greats. Then I could retort, "Thank you. That's the nicest thing anyone's ever said to me." But that just wasn't in my cards.

I knew Roger Staubach had retired the year before, and I couldn't resist needling him as we ran side-by-side.

"Aren't you supposed to be playing today?" I asked with a grin.

He smiled back and said, "I decided this would be better exercise." Then he sped up, and I lost him in the crowd of runners.

Later, after the race and Thanksgiving brunch, we all congregated around the television to watch the Cowboys game. I told everyone about my Roger Staubach moment, and we all shared a laugh.

It was one of my grandmother's final Thanksgivings with us. We'd been noticing that she was struggling with memory issues, but we dismissed it.

"She forgets everything," we'd shake our heads and shrug, believing that this was normal behavior for an elderly woman. There wasn't much information about dementia or Alzheimer's back then, so it was easy to ignore the more serious implications of her memory loss.

It became clear that Mommy was slowly moving into the early stages of cognitive decline. There came a day when we had to take her car keys away, and that just about broke her spirit. She knew that if she couldn't drive, her entire life would be lost forever. Driving was how she got to church, her social activities, and charity work. It was akin to taking away her right to practice her religion or vote.

As her dementia progressed, she wrote notes to remind herself of what she was supposed to do and who she was supposed to know, writing them in pencil just in case she needed to change the words. She even put notes in the cabinet to remind herself to get a drinking glass or plate for her food. Soon, the notes she left herself were largely illegible.

My mom cared for her the best that she could until our grandmother made her transition during her 95th year. Setting our differences aside, this was a heart-wrenching death to witness. I saw how Alzheimer's empties a person's most prized possession – their sweet memories – and strips them of their independence.

> *"Alzheimer's is the cleverest thief, because she not only steals from you, but she steals the very thing you need to remember what's been stolen."*
>
> **Jarod Kintz**

Around this time, my mom was ready to retire from Republic National Bank, the largest bank in Dallas at the time. During her illustrious 46-year career, she worked her way up from a bank teller position to a Vice President. She knew everyone – from the CEO to the janitors – and she was liked by them all. Mom also served a few terms as President of the Dallas Credit Women's Association, and was known as a leader, as well as a terrific speaker with wonderful stage presence.

I saw it firsthand. As a young boy, I would take the bus and go to the bank to meet her, and she'd give me a little money to see a movie at the nearby Majestic Theater. The way her colleagues said her name and the tone they used when speaking to her showed me how they respected her and valued her presence.

Her retirement party was well-attended, and all her friends from the bank and the Dallas Credit Women's Association showed up to shower mom and her family with love and well wishes. The CEO and President of her bank – Jim Barry and Charles Pister, respectively – made glowing speeches, paid their respects, and gave Mom an award for being the longest tenured employee to ever work at the bank. She was also given a wildly extravagant Neiman Marcus gift certificate to spend however she chose. I will never forget how proud she looked that day.

The big question everyone asked her was, "What's next?"

My mom didn't hesitate in her answer: "I want to travel to seven continents."

She always followed through on her goals. She soon learned that her favorite places to travel were Hong Kong, London, and Australia, with Antarctica coming in a close fourth. My mom was a volunteer with her time, devoting much of it to her favorite charities, but she also carved out some to learn arts and crafts. Someone along the way told her she wasn't creative, or maybe that's the story she told herself, but she certainly changed that perception!

> *Creativity is a natural*
> *extension of our enthusiasm.*
>
> **Earl Nightingale**

I can't help but shake my head at all she accomplished, and I had a front-row seat to it all. Working three jobs just to keep food on the table, raising three children on her own, and becoming the first female Vice President in the Dallas banking community was impressive enough. But she also ended up a millionaire!

Proud isn't a big enough word to describe how I felt about this woman. I am endlessly grateful for the life she gave me, and the one she showed me.

To me, she was worth ten Roger Staubachs.

Chapter Fifteen
Flying High

My career with Fast-Tax continued to rise, and my territory changed from the Western part of the country to the Northeast after a team shift left the region in need of a sales rep. I was happy to include New York in my domain because that's the city with the largest money center banks; my earning potential increased immediately.

New York excited me to no end. I had been a tourist a few times when I'd attend banking conventions, so I knew my way around the parts of town I'd need to know. Far from an expert, I still knew how to hail a taxi in the rain and find the most discerning wine retailers in the city. Is there more to New York?

Yes. So much more. Visually, my eyes never stopped working; they took in the skyscrapers huddled tightly, one after another, long city blocks teeming with crowds no matter what time of day, impatient cars and buses, and blaring sirens cutting through it all. There was bustling uptown, midtown, downtown, and the fresh green respite Central Park provided just when you didn't feel like seeing any more concrete and glass. I took in Broadway, Carnegie Hall, and the Metropolitan Museum of Art, and I can't begin to list all the restaurants and delicious meals I enjoyed, no matter my craving or the time.

> *"I love New York. You can pop out of the Underworld in Central Park, hail a taxi, head down Fifth Avenue with a giant hellhound loping behind you, and nobody even looks at you funny."*
>
> **Rick Riordan**

It wasn't all easy; on my first subway ride, I got lost and ended up in the Bronx on sixth trillionth street.

On one of my trips to the Big Apple, my mentor John joined me for an important meeting with the largest trust department in the country. It went well; I made sure my pants were fastened, I didn't comment on anyone's facial features, and no one screamed at me. We made our way down the elevator, through the lobby, and out to the street to hail taxis. While we waited, we talked intently about the meeting, brainstorming about our next steps.

"Okay," John said. "I need to get downtown for another meeting."

"I'm going to the hotel to check in," I told him. "I'll see you there later."

John got into his taxi just as mine pulled over. I had just thrown my garment bag and briefcase into the back seat of the taxi when a man with a helpful look on his face approached me.

"Is that your money?" he asked, pointing down at the ground.

I looked down for a half-second and saw two dollars on the ground. "Nope," I answered, suddenly noticing activity on the other side of my taxi.

"Hey!" I yelled at a man reaching inside the passenger door, clearly trying to steal my luggage.

The taxi driver, obviously accustomed to New York shenanigans, hopped out to subdue the man who had tried to sway my attention with the "Is that your money" ruse, while I was in a tug-of-war contest with the luggage thief.

"LET GO!" I screamed, startling the guy so much that he dropped my suitcase in the street and ran off.

And that is how I happened to be picking up all of my garments I'd packed for the week – including underwear, socks, suits, and ties – off of Fifth Avenue, right in front of Tiffany's. I consider that my Welcome to New York moment.

Over breakfast the next morning, John and I talked more about the sales call the previous day.

"Converting the largest trust department's business from our main competitor to Fast-Tax is a long shot," he said.

"Well, did you hear him mention that he was retiring next year?" I asked. The head of the department had been a fixture at the company for 42 years, and my guess was that he wasn't about to change things up before he left.

John knew exactly what I was thinking, and suggested we wait until his departure to attempt to win their business.

"You've got a much better relationship with his second-in-command," he noted. "And she's more open to change."

I liked brainstorming with John because he didn't do a lot of hand-wringing; if he had a problem, he researched potential solutions until he was able to make a decision in which he had unwavering faith.

"So I met with my financial planner a while back," he started, telling me all about his retirement plan. "And he asked me what I was planning on doing after I leave the workforce."

John held out his arms like he couldn't believe the question.

"And I told him, 'I have no idea!'"

So what did John do? He researched, talking to family and friends, some of whom had retired without a plan of what to do next, and eventually hired a career coach to provide some clarity. After just a few sessions, he realized that the answer became evident as soon as he aligned himself with what he valued most: his future should have something to do with teaching and learning. It definitely got me thinking...

I continued the conversation when I returned home, asking my mother for her opinions and expertise. Having such a proven businessperson in my house never failed to impress me. I've said it before, but I think I won the mom lottery.

After I told her all about John's plan, I said, "I know a few things for certain. One, I want the freedom to do what I want, whenever I want. And two, I really enjoy helping people improve their performance and become the best version of themselves."

"I think you'd make an amazing people coach," she nodded. That validation was all I needed.

I decided then and there to upgrade my coaching skills.

> *"The decision to change direction in life can be made in an instant, but the process of actually changing your mindset may take months or years."*
>
> **Dr. Nathan Mellor**

The next time John and I traveled together, he asked if I wanted to see his retirement plan. I was interested in investing and started by putting money into my 401k in 1983, three years after the program was available to American companies and their workers.

"Sure," I said, genuinely interested.

He whipped out his computer and showed me a spreadsheet containing a bunch of numbers.

"If I have a four percent withdrawal rate each year from my taxable and non-taxable investments, I'm good," John figured. "My plan is to go back to school, get my PhD, become a professor, and teach geology."

I was impressed. He was putting himself in position to teach and learn, his most meaningful values. This idea of what I valued resonated with me for many years.

In the meantime, I grinded. For seven consecutive years, I was a President's Club qualifier at Fast-Tax because of my sales performance. I even managed to earn Top Sales Leader of the Year for two consecutive years in a row. But I take great pride that I helped so many of my peers along the way, pushing them to become sales leaders themselves and advance their own careers into management positions.

My success got the attention of recruiters who specialized in high tech sales. I was getting calls practically every day to find out if I might be interested in making a change to another company, but most of the opportunities were not as good as I had it at Fast-Tax.

One day, however, I got a call from a recruiter by the name of Ralph.

"You ever think about moving to enterprise software sales?" he asked, telling me that the top sales leader at Dun & Bradstreet Software made $500,000 the year before, which was almost three times what I was earning.

He got my attention.

Ralph got me an interview with one of the sales managers at D&B, but I didn't measure up in terms of experience with the other candidates. I simply didn't have experience selling enterprise wide financial and manufacturing systems, and they did.

"Listen," Ralph said. "The sales manager was really impressed with you, so you never know..."

A year later, that same sales manager left D&B and went to work for Oracle Corporation.

Oracle was known mostly for its relational database, the way that computer systems store and access information. It started with $2,000 of its own funding, $1,200 of which came from one of its founders, the incredibly interesting and flamboyant Larry Ellison. He's known for trash-talking his competitors, and was always in the news for taking up yet another expensive hobby – like yacht racing or buying a Hawaiian island and turning it into a wellness utopia and green community. At the time, Oracle was just entering the business of developing enterprise applications to compete with D&B and a German company called SAP.

Ralph called and asked if I'd be interested in an interview with the Oracle sales manager, and I jumped at the opportunity. She and I hit it off straight away, and she truly seemed to appreciate that I had a method to my sales process and that I had developed a ROI tool to woo customers to Fast-Tax.

"I'd love you to join our team," she told me.

> *"You have to act, and act now."*
>
> **Larry Ellison**

The financial package at Oracle was substantially higher than what I was earning at Fast-Tax, but Fast-Tax was safe and reliable; Oracle was known as an aggressive sales organization that fired people if they did not meet their quotas. But I was at a time in my career when I wanted to challenge myself, and safe and reliable wasn't cutting it anymore. I agreed to their offer, and gave my resignation to Fast-Tax.

I dreaded telling John. I shouldn't have been surprised that he offered me all his blessings on my new venture.

"Hey, I'm surprised it has taken this long for you to begin searching for a new home," John said.

Honestly, he was one of the biggest reasons I stayed for so long. He had been my manager, mentor, and good friend for the last seven years. My life changed for the better the day he asked me, "How would you like to make some real money?"

John afforded me the opportunity to grow as a sales leader and as a person. As a result of his intervention and interest, I got to travel to 45 states and see so much of this beautiful country of ours. I was successful on the West coast, the East coast, and everywhere in between, but I do credit my time in the always-challenging New York with maturing me professionally and personally. They're right when they say, "If I can make it there, I'll make it anywhere."

Sure, the travel led to my marital demise, but the good definitely outweighed the bad. As I tried for most of my life, I chose to look at the positives instead.

Before I started my new gig at Oracle, I went to see my old pal Travis, who now lived in Anchorage, Alaska. Soon after college, Travis and his family had moved to Alaska to seek greater fortunes and enjoy the great outdoors. Some of my best memories included him, and I wanted to get together to make another one.

We'd formed a natural bond as captains of our high school football team, and I counted him among my best friends. I remember playing next to him during our most important football game of the year as I got run over again and again by massive linemen with missing teeth and bad breath. No matter what I tried, they blocked me on every running play.

"I'm getting killed!" I yelled to Travis. "I can't stop them!"

Then there were our adventures in his purple Volkswagen, our drunken brawl in high school, and my motorcycle accident. Every time I was with Travis, I either had the time of my life, or experienced a life lesson. I hope everyone has a Travis in their memory bank.

Growing up, Travis' mom was a nurse, and his dad Herman was a man of many talents. Herman fought in the Korean War, was a good father, an artist, pilot, and terrific mechanic; he could fix just about anything. He also loved anything to do with the outdoors, including camping, hunting, and fishing, and passed down that trait to Travis.

My family liked Travis because he had this approachable temperament and his personality, well, it was as big as Texas. My sister said he had bedroom eyes.

Travis reserved a guided trip for us to fish for halibut in the infamous Cook Inlet, named after Captain Cook by George Vancouver who served under Cook in the British Navy. Cook was a legendary naval captain and explorer of the Canadian coastline that borders Alaska.

The thing about halibut fishing is that they swim close to the bottom of the ocean, so you have to weigh down your lines to get the bait to the bottom. We were using three-pound weights, bobbing them up and down for long periods of time. By the end of the day, our biceps looked like Sylvester Stallone's!

We caught 14 halibut that day, which was our limit. In total we caught about 500 pounds of halibut, which was twice the weight of big ole Travis. Two of the halibut were over 115 pounds apiece! To prevent the larger fish from breaking our legs with their tails when we got them on the boat, the guide used a shotgun to put them to sleep.

Before our flight to Anchorage, the guides removed the skin from the fish to try to lessen their weight, but it didn't make a big enough difference; the three of us and the fish were still 150 pounds over the required weight limit of Herman's aircraft.

While we waited on the runway, I could see a large tree line in the distance that our plane had to clear. Herman could not get enough altitude on our first attempt, and aborted the takeoff.

"The simple fact is this: when you go to Alaska, you get your ass kicked."

Mark Twight

"How are we going to make it over those trees?" I worriedly asked Herman.

He shrugged and laughed, "I guess we'll just have to leave Travis behind!"

In all seriousness, he gave us his real plan. "I'm going to need you and Travis to lean forward as far as possible until we scale that tree line. Hopefully, that will equalize the weight from front to back."

It worked, but I realized in that moment that *hopefully* is one of the most frightening words to hear in life. Especially when you're flying.

Chapter Sixteen
Working the Oracle

It was 11:30 pm, just a short half-hour until the day turned into tomorrow. My boss Matt, who was the Vice President of Sales for the region, and I were huddled together at his desk trying to close a $3 million enterprise software deal ($5 million in today's dollars) with a division of a Top Five semiconductor company. Getting a signed contract from them before 11:59 pm would enable our area to make its sales number for the rest of the year.

We were in tense negotiations with the company's Chief Information Officer, who I coincidentally helped get the job. In her previous employment, she also used our technology and was an enormous fan of Oracle solutions, and wanted her current employer to have the same systems.

We agreed wholeheartedly with her on that matter, but she was miffed that we were holding firm on the number of user licenses that she could have. Keep in mind that this deal was taking place before SaaS or Cloud services.

> *"If there is no disparity of opinions, there is nothing of value being discussed."*
>
> **Vineet Raj Kapoor**

"We can't meet that number," I told her. "We just can't."

We did not have a choice; if we acquiesced to what she wanted, it would be more than what we had negotiated with another division in the same company.

The clock kept ticking. Finally, at 11:55 pm, we reached an agreement to split the difference between the CIO's wishes and our position, committing to dealing with the internal power struggles after the contract was executed. We held our breath until we received the fax of the signed contract at exactly 11:58 pm. Once we had reviewed the fax and guaranteed that it was legitimate, we started jumping around like kids on a trampoline.

We yelled, "We did it! We did it!" And the celebration commenced!

That deal sealed it: our area had made its numbers for the year. I represented 405% of increased sales, which positioned me to be named the Enterprise Sales Leader of the year, worldwide, for the second-largest software company on the planet. It was the second year in a row that I had achieved such lofty sales numbers.

Oracle was a prestigious organization, and I felt honored to walk into a sales meeting representing them. I had instant credibility when I announced myself to the receptionist: "Bruce McCombs. Oracle."

But honestly, it was also the most difficult work that I'd ever done before. To be fair, driving that dump truck back in the day was a much sweatier, more laborious job, but this one was mentally taxing. It was complicated, especially the number of steps involved in winning sales contracts.

The number of people to whom I could potentially sell had also increased dramatically, which seemed like a good thing – and it was! But earning potential aside, all of these people had different agendas and a "What's in it for me" type of attitude that could be challenging to navigate.

I'm a process guy – there's *always* a method to my madness – and so I started thinking of concrete, streamlined ways to manage my clients' different agendas. Eventually, I landed on a solution and called it the Sales Navigation System (SNS).

The SNS is all about predictable outcomes. The SNS helped develop a map to an agreed-upon destination or objective, and enabled me to adequately answer the question, "What steps do I have to go through to close more business deals?" In turn, the SNS methodology enabled the prospect to buy into the process because they saw the benefits of fewer surprises.

Close your eyes and imagine a sales campaign with few surprises. That's nearly impossible, right?

Not exactly.

> *"The expected always happens."*
>
> **Benjamin Disraeli**

Essentially, the SNS is an event calendar for the evaluation, selection, and implementation of solutions you're selling to the buyer. It acts as a clear roadmap to an agreed-upon destination or objective, and it helps the sales leader manage expectations with the buyer so that there are very few – if any – surprises throughout the sales campaign. There's no need for fire extinguishers or heated email exchanges that begin with "Per my last email..." or apologies for miscommunication. It's about helping the customer solve problems.

My objective was to have a buyer live on a new system within an agreed-upon time frame, meaning that all users are fully trained and there's no more use for their old system.

I've learned that sales – and any relationship – depends on clear communication. So I designed the SNS to be a communication tool for the sales leader with managing the delivery of their vision, easily enabling their sales team to execute their plan. As we progressed deeper into the SNS, it's a terrific test that the sale is advancing, and trust is building.

Before the buyer proceeded with the evaluation, I tried to get the VIP to sign a letter that outlines the steps to which we've all agreed. This was a tall task because companies did not want to lose control of the evaluation. However, when it worked, getting signatures is particularly appropriate when the deal is exclusive, and the company has agreed to evaluate your solution only. My signatory letter went something like the example on the following page.

Mr. John Doe
CFO
ABC Company
2130 Cedar View
Mission Hills, CO 92678

Dear Mr. Doe:

As we have discussed, we employ a sequence of events for the evaluation, selection, and installation of ABC's solutions. The key benefit of the sequence of events (attached) is that it acts as a clear roadmap to an agreed-upon destination, or objective. That objective is to have ABC live on a new system within an agreed-upon time frame, meaning that all users are fully trained, and your company is now completely independent of your old system.

The sequence of events is beneficial because it enables you to begin with the end. It outlines the necessary steps and benchmarks involved to being live on your new system within the parameters we've set. The sequence of events is a dynamic tool at this stage and is merely a blueprint to help us stay focused as the project progresses; I'm sure it will go through some fine-tuning and revisions as we proceed deeper into the project.

Of particular importance: The go/no go decision is crucial every time. Unless we agree on a satisfactory conclusion for each benchmark, we will not move on to the next step. This process will set proper expectations while eliminating as many surprises as possible. Unless we're talking about birthday parties and lottery tickets, we don't like surprises!

Before we proceed with the evaluation, we like to ensure that everyone involved agrees with our proposed sequencing, which you'll find below. After your review and signature, we can begin.

I am looking forward to providing ABC Company with the best solutions and service XYZ Corporation has to offer. If you have any questions, please reach out.

Sincerely,
Jim Nassium
Senior Director Sales
Enclosure

____________________________ ____________________

John Doe (CFO) Date

Company ABC Sequence of Events

Date	**Activity**	**Go/No Go**
4/2	Introductory Visit	GO
4/16	Survey Requirements	
4/30	Demonstration	
5/30	Customer Reference Site Visit	
6/30	Present Business Case	
7/15	ABC recommends XYZ Corporation	
8/30	Propose/Negotiate/Legal Red Lines	
9/30	Execute Agreement	
10/30	Implementation/Training begins	

I soon learned that even though the SNS was intended for use by sales leaders and their prospective customers, it was an extremely flexible model that could be adapted to achieve *any* personal or professional life goal. It is a brilliant tool, and I'd even make that claim if one of my colleagues created it! (Except for my Napoleonic manager at Fast-Tax. Although, to be perfectly honest, I am uncertain he'd be able to create anything to help make others' jobs and lives easier!)

While Fast-Tax showed me the US, Oracle showed me the world. I ended up spending a lot of time in Europe, which wasn't bad at all – especially the wineries!

One of my fondest memories was my stay at the terrific Borgo San Felicia winery located in Castelnuovo Berardenga, Italy, in the heart of the Chianti wine region. The resort is restored in 8th Century buildings surrounded by 140 hectares of vineyards, featuring accents such as stone walls, terracotta tile floors, and exposed wooden beams. It was the perfect blend of old world meets luxe, with serene private patios off of every suite, a romantic piano bar with unparalleled décor and service, two restaurants specializing in Tuscan cuisine, and all the spa and fitness amenities you could imagine.

San Felicia's 5-Star restaurants served gourmet food that included wild boar and roasted pigeon. I had never eaten either of these delicacies before my visit, and I found both to be quite gamey. Regardless, the rest of the food paired beautifully with the San Felicia lineup of unforgettable wines, from Chianti to Brunello Montalcino. Every morning, we were served a lovely spread for breakfast, and then I lounged by the pool. It was the start of October, and the temperature was perfect. My heart rate settles just recalling it all.

> *"Life without wine would be like an ocean without water."*
>
> **Angelo De Fazio**

Just a few miles down the road from San Felicia, Tenuta di Arceno is an ancient Tuscan estate originally planted in 1504 with a diverse portfolio of wines. Three of their wines centered on the native Sangiovese grape in the Chianti Classico collection, and another three celebrated the estate's international varieties under the Toscana designation. The vineyard has gone through a few ownership changes over the years, but Jess Jackson, California's famous wine visionary, purchased the estate in the 1990s and established Tenuta di Arceno with wine maker Pierre Seillan. Located near the fork of two rivers, this area was formerly the nexus of the Etruscan civilization. Etruscans preceded the Romans, and then intermixed with them when the Romans took control of the region. In honor of its history, the reference to *arceno* comes from the Etruscan word *arkhé*, meaning *point of origin*.

Before Jess bought the property, all visits were by appointment only. That changed immediately with the establishment of regular hours of operation, Monday through Friday, as he worked toward his goal of making Tenuta di Arceno feel as welcome as a California winery. They started serving prosciutto and other assorted meats and gourmet Italian cheeses with the tastings, too, and soon enough their reputation soared. One of their wines earned number 19 in the Wine Spectator's Top 100 wines in the early 2000s.

I also visited Venice, that beautiful city on the water, to meet up with my colleagues from Oracle. We had all qualified for membership in the exclusive President's Club, hosted by the President/COO of Oracle.

Our agenda included a masquerade ball and concert featuring David Sanborn, the infamous jazz great.

I bought a Casanova black cape and mask as my costume for the ball. I'd always been fascinated by his legend. Giacomo Girolamo Casanova grew up in Venice in the mid 1700s, and the world equates his name with his purported affairs with many, many women. But there was so much more to him that intrigued me. For instance, he entered university at the age of 12 and graduated at 17 with a law degree, which blew my mind; you already know what I was doing during my teenage years! Casanova was also a world traveler, violinist, diplomat, and self-proclaimed knight. Yes, he proclaimed himself Knight of Seingalt! He lived an intense life, associating with European royalty, popes, and artistic figures such as Voltaire and Mozart, and spent his last years as a librarian. He also proclaimed himself to be a...well...Casanova, writing an autobiography that details every woman he seduced – around 120 in all.

So, he and I were incredibly similar. (I hope that elicited a laugh!)

My Casanova getup was a hit at the masquerade ball, and my outfit won the best costume award of the night. The unforgettable evening ended with a fantastic firework display on the backdrop of the Adriatic Sea.

The next night was the Awards Dinner, where I was named as the number one sales leader for Oracle worldwide. What an honor, and what a trophy; it was a stunning hand-blown glass piece from the famous Murano glass house, Antica Vetreria Fratelli Toso. I keep that award on display in a trophy case, mostly as a reminder of the good old days but also as a memento of hard work and overcoming self doubt.

That evening, we were treated to a Diana Ross concert, the lead singer of the Supremes. She almost didn't make it, as she experienced a bit of a hassle with the Custom Authority when she tried to enter Italy. You wouldn't have known it; she performed beautifully, and was charming and engaging with the crowd. There were moments when I couldn't believe I was experiencing this evening.

Luckily, I enjoyed the high times while they lasted; the following year's President's Club trip was definitely scaled back. Apparently, Oracle's President and Larry Ellison had differences of opinion about how the company should be run, and he was forced out.

We ended up celebrating in Germany, which was still a beautiful country with an incredibly rich history. Munich was our home base, so when we weren't touring castles and playing Octoberfest games, you could find us at the Marienplatz, which has been the city's main square since 1158. It was exactly as I'd pictured it: amusing albeit mildly annoying mimes, thousands of people touristing, and lots of beer. The beer wasn't at all surprising; Munich is home to the world's oldest brewery still in action, dating back to 700 AD.

Hall and Oats was the main musical attraction at the Awards Dinner, and they had the whole place jamming to their tunes. I'd enjoyed another stellar year, achieving 385% of the sales quota, placing me at the top of leaderboard.

After the club trip, I detoured to the wine region of Alsace, an historical region in northeastern France on the Rhine River. Bordering Germany and Switzerland, it has alternated between German and French control over the centuries, and reflects a mix of those two cultures. Its capital, Strasbourg, is centered on the Ill River's Grand Île island, bordered by canals and home to the Gothic Cathédrale Notre-Dame de Strasbourg. Alsace is famous for its beer, sauerkraut, and white wines including Gewurztraminer, Riesling, and Pinot Gris. During my stay, I ate at Michelin 2-Star restaurant called JY's, named after the owner's first name, Jean-Yves.

Alsace is known for having the most Michelin Star restaurants in France, and I imagine that has a lot to do with its location and the rotating mix of cultural influences. It's both a traditional and inventive setting, a feat very few dining establishments achieve – much less an entire region of them.

I ordered poached salmon, and the sommelier expertly suggested a beautiful Pinot Noir. Every morsel of food I ate, I had to put my fork down so I could enjoy each bite because it was so rich. This entire experience was so far from my Boone's Farm misadventure, and I know the younger me would be just as amazed as I was at that dinner.

The next day, I drove to Paris to spend a few days in the city. In the 17th century, King Louis XIV wanted the city to be known as a safe place for residents and travelers alike. His creative solution was to install lanterns on every street corner and encourage residents to light candles in their windows. Almost overnight, the city became known as The City of Lights.

The next few days, I toured the Louvre, Versailles, climbed to the top of the Eiffel Tower, and attended Mass at Notre Dame. There was beauty everywhere I looked, so much so that it was overwhelming at times.

I really enjoyed the Sacré-Coeur Basilica, often simply called Sacré-Coeur, a Roman Catholic church dedicated to the Sacred Heart of Jesus. The church is made from travertine limestone and is located at the summit of the Montmartre, the second-highest point in the city after the Eiffel Tower. Even before its construction, this location was chosen by believers to be a holy spot because, in their estimation, it was the closest to Heaven and God. It's a visually impressive structure, and the church bell alone is worth a visit. It took 21 horses to drag the 19-ton bell to the top of Montmartre back in 1895, and it remains one of the biggest and heaviest bells in the world.

I found my next experience by happenstance, following the back streets until I spotted a sign for a Picasso hangout. Then I walked past the former living quarters of Renoir and Van Gogh, imagining how different life must've been for them. At the bottom of the hill was Moulin Rouge, the famous cabaret. I learned a few things about that spot beyond the legendary Cancan, including the fact that it was the first building in Paris to have electricity! The entire area was filled with artists and their easels, painting landscapes and still portraits one after the other.

There were moments during my travel when I had to stop and shake my head a little, amazed at how far I'd come in life. Having the opportunity to see such sights, eat such meals, and experience such diverse cultures was an honor that was not lost on me.

But despite these opportunities, awards, and attention, I think I would always have that part of me that believed I wasn't worthy of any of it.

Chapter Seventeen
Back to Reality

Real life hit as soon as I returned home from Europe. Steve, one of my closest friends from childhood and the bass player in The Dimensions, called to let me know he was diagnosed with liver disease.

"It's not great news," he told me. "My doctor says I've got only a few weeks left...and I'd really like to get together with you and the other guys. And I really want to apologize for how I acted the last time we saw each other."

I had not seen nor talked to Steve in over year. The last time I saw him, things got a bit heated. I had a friend at the house who was helping me learn woodworking and adding his expertise to blueprints for a wine cellar I was building. Steve popped in unannounced, clearly under the influence of drugs or alcohol – or both. He was agitated and aggressive, and every other word out of his mouth was an F-bomb.

My friend and I tried to ignore his behavior, but he kept interrupting us and asking if we had any cocaine.

Now, I'd seen Steve under the influence before, but this time was different. He was so blasted that he was unable to discern right from wrong.

"Hey, buddy," I said, pulling him aside. "Why don't you sleep this off in my guest room?"

He wasn't having it, and I had to ask him to leave.

But all was forgiven in an instant.

"I'll round up everyone, and we'll be there," I told him.

So Chuck, Bill, Louis, and I piled into Eddy's white SUV and drove out to Steve's home in Longview, 115 miles east of Dallas. It was horrible to see my friend looking so jaundiced and emaciated, with a swollen, distended belly from his diseased liver.

We were all heartbroken that one of our best childhood friends was suffering so much, but we picked up right where we left off, reminiscing about our old band, playing cards, golf, and all the hilarious stories we'd almost forgotten. After a couple of really enjoyable hours, we said our farewells to Steve and his family. A few weeks later, Steve's wife called to tell me that he died in his nurse's arms.

> *"The story of life is quicker than the wink of an eye, the story of love is hello and goodbye... until we meet again."*
>
> **Jimi Hendrix**

I really believe the die was cast for Steve early in his childhood. His parents were alcoholics, and their example set Steve up to also be an alcoholic. No matter how much we tried to encourage him to seek medical help, he always had an excuse as to why he couldn't stop or why he didn't need help. His addiction was one of the most frustrating things I've ever experienced.

Steve's final wishes were that his family and close friends disperse his ashes on beautiful Stevens Park golf course. And so, we assembled at the 3rd golf hole, three houses down from where Steve grew up, dug our hands into the urn that held Steve's ashes, and generously spread them on the putting surface. After the ceremony, we convened at my house to enjoy food and beverages before we started a card game. It was all just like Steve would have wanted.

I had not been back to work since I returned from my overseas tour. My desk was packed with unopened mail, and my inbox was the same. I sat down to tackle some of it, seriously contemplating the *delete all* function, when one subject line caught my eye: Are You Happy on Mondays?

To be perfectly honest, I've never been a fan of Mondays. Even as my jobs got more exciting and profitable, I still dragged my feet on Sunday nights. It was just hard for me to find Monday motivation. I guess I was more of a weekend kind of guy.

That was the only email I opened that morning. Inside, it asked the question, "What do you call people who are happy on Mondays?"

The answer? Retired.

I couldn't help but remember the conversations between me and my old Fast-Tax manager, John. He'd viewed retirement as the time in his life to actually live his life the way he'd always dreamed of living it.

Why not live like that now? I thought. I knew that I did not want to be selling enterprise software until I reached Rip Van Winkle's age; the travel was hectic and the constant stress to perform better than everyone around me was affecting my health. That said, I had just enjoyed two of my best earning years at Oracle, and there was no reason this next year wouldn't be equally prosperous. No matter how much I wanted to be happy on Mondays, I couldn't turn my back on the money. Long airport security lines, fried airport food, and interrupted relationships would be my reality until I could.

Eventually, my success at Oracle forced me into a management role. After yet another reorganization, my new boss told me that the only role left in her organization for me was overseeing top-performing sales leaders. Take it or leave it.

> *"Leaders set the direction, build an inspiring vision where they want to go, and create a path for others to follow."*
>
> **Bruce McCombs**

I was the natural choice. I'd done the job and done it well, and had also shown a propensity for helping others find their true potential and succeed. I wasn't stingy with my success, and always felt that *everyone* should be thriving. Plus, she'd already spoken to the individuals who would report to me, and they reviewed me and my track record effusively.

I also had a niggling thought that she wanted me in a management position in Dallas so that she wouldn't be forced to travel back and forth from California to check on us. Since she already knew the team was excited to have me at the helm, Dallas would be one less worry on her list.

I accepted the management position, and tried my best to set the direction, create a vision, and motivate my team. A few of my sales leaders went on to management roles and I hope created a path for them to follow. But after a while, I got the sales bug again and was able to move back to my old role of sales leader. This time, I was armed with all the things I learned during my time managing others, which led me to prosper and achieve more than I'd ever dreamed possible.

Looking back at my Oracle stats, I can't help but give myself a well-earned pat on the back. I'd achieved at least 90% of my sales quota during my sales career. Through the years, I'd ranked Number One and Number Three on the Sales Leaderboard worldwide. I'd sold over $170 million in software through sales and professional services. Not bad for a guy from Oak Cliff, Texas.

All those years, though, that emailed question floated to the surface every once in a while: What do you call people who are happy on Mondays?

I continued to wrestle with the concept of finally aligning myself with my true values or continuing to chase wealth. I had invested in my 401k early while at Fast-Tax. I also met a financial adviser who I trusted. Chris taught me the importance of diversifying my financial portfolio, trading financial instruments, and building a municipal bond ladder to lower my taxes and fund my retirement.

I can certainly retire from Oracle and live comfortably, I thought. *What am I waiting for?*

So I started to really map out what my new career would look like, and researched some coaching schools. Oddly, I was drawn to one in particular that was based just outside San Francisco. I couldn't help but think of Crystal, that palm reader from my younger years, who predicted that my future could be found on the West coast with a bottle in my hand.

> *"If you ask what is one of the most enjoyable things in this world, I would say that it is surprising people suddenly and in an extraordinary way!"*
>
> **Mehmet Murat Ildan**

"I'm resigning."

I'd researched long enough. I knew my plan was to leave Oracle and pursue a coaching career, but I didn't really know I'd be telling my manager *that* day. I don't know how to explain it, other than I felt compelled to change my day-to-day. And I must've thought that there's no time like the present!

I caught her completely off guard. She spilled her coffee on her white blouse, trying to dab the stain while trying to catch her breath. Finally, once the commotion died down and the shock wore off, she asked, "But why?"

"It's time," I said. "And I've found an opportunity that offers freedom...no travel...no sales quotas...and I can conduct business from anywhere in the world, on *my* schedule."

"Oh," she thought about it for a half-second. "Can you hire me?"

In between Oracle and starting my coaching practice, I wrote Robert Mondavi a letter about my experience at his winery in the 70s. I was making big life moves, and I seriously thought about buying property in Napa, trying my hand at winemaking. As we all know, Mr. Mondavi was a pioneer in the industry, and had a significant influence on the quality and innovation of viticulture in California. If I was seeking someone's guidance, I wanted to be sure it was guidance from the best in the business!

He responded with a personal letter, apologizing that he would be unable to meet.

I'll be in New York at the time of your visit, he wrote. *But I would like you to meet with David, my Chief of Operations.*

For the second time, twenty years since the first, I walked under the archway that leads into the Mondavi property. It was just as I remembered: warm, welcoming, and setting the standard for California vineyards.

David met me in the front and after a few pleasantries, we made our way to a table that overlooked the famous To Kalon vineyard. It was breathtaking; rows upon rows of verdant vines in perfect order, with that unmistakable red oxidized earth beneath them. Place of the Highest Beauty, indeed.

We chatted a bit before I got down to business. "How much money would I need to invest in property, and how many plantable acres I would need to be successful?"

His answer was certainly more than I had invested at the time. I continued to ask questions that I had prepared because I did not want to spoil the generosity of the winery and the wonderful experience that I was having.

After lunch, David escorted me to the tasting room where he had lined up five Reserve To Kalon glasses of wine for me to taste. The years of the wine ranged from the 1970s to the mid 1990s. It was an absolute delight. The 100% cabernet had low tannins, great nose, and still had a smooth, yet powerful finish. I bought three of the wines and mailed them to my home address.

That lunch was quite an experience. The scenery was fabulous, the food was delicious, and the wines were very special. David's hospitality and customer service were terrific, as well. I still often reach for Mondavi To Kalon Cabernet Reserve when I can find it.

After Mondavi, I had wine tasting reservations at Spottswoode Winery down the road to taste their beautiful cabernets. I got out of the car, walked up the sidewalk to the door, and knocked on it several times. No one answered. I even walked around the back of the house to see if anyone was home. Alas, I had gotten stood up. I left a note on the door, letting them know I was sorry to have missed the tasting.

I received a package from Spottswoode a few days after I got home from my trip. They'd sent six bottles of their top cabernet sauvignon, along with a note from Tony, Spottswoode's winemaker. The note read: *I am so sorry that I was not available for your tasting. I hope this gift will make up for it!*

It did. His kindness and generosity left their mark, and I've followed Tony's trajectory ever since. He now owns his own winery in Oregon, producing highly-reviewed wines under his own label.

I learned a lot from my interactions at the various vineyards, and I recognized the parallels between a sales leader and a winemaker. They both have to respect the process, maintain quality throughout, and build a trusted, likable reputation.

Let the coaching begin.

Chapter Eighteen
Put Me In, Coach

There's nothing quite like the exhilaration and inspiration that comes home with us after a fantastic trip. I had just tasted a new part of the world, and I wanted it for breakfast, lunch, and dinner, and every snack in between. Boy, I couldn't wait to get started on my new career.

But ask anyone to tell you their number one stressor in their life, and an overwhelming majority will answer, "Work. Definitely work."

So, along with all of those positive emotions, I definitely felt panic, too. *What if I fail? What if I should've stayed with Oracle? What if I miss the insane amount of money they were throwing my way? What if I fail?*

Yep. Failure was the concern, for sure.

> *"There is only one thing that makes a dream impossible to achieve: the fear of failure."*
>
> **Paulo Coelho**

I've learned throughout my career that when uncertainty hits, it's integral to remind yourself of the realities. For me, I needed to remember that I had always been successful in my job trajectories; from the time I left my very first job, I'd always bettered my pay and work environment. That was an undisputable fact.

In addition, I followed the sharp advice of the greatest businessperson I'd ever known, who advised me that I wouldn't go wrong if I was the hardest worker in any room, and if I stayed humble. Thanks for that one, Mom.

I also knew that it is extremely important to prepare for the future I wanted, so I threw myself into searching for the right program to fit my goals, making sure that it was certified by the International Coaching Institute (ICF). Like I mentioned earlier, one stood out more than the rest: The Co-Active Training Institute, based just outside San Francisco.

Thomas Leonard is credited as the father of life coaching. Originally a financial planner, he realized that his clients needed more than financial tips to address their varying levels of ineffective behaviors and stalled progress. He found that his clients were not only in need of a spiritual, physical, and emotional reset, they *craved* it. His coaching touched on relationship issues, family and friend boundaries, health goals, and setting aside time for leisure and fun. Over time, his clients reached their full potential, and the enthusiasm for life coaching spread like wildfire. That was over 40 years ago, but it remains a game-changer for those searching for betterment.

Leonard started CoachU, the first coaching school where students enrolled in classes to learn how to guide others toward success. His groundbreaking book, *The Portable Coach*, is a treatise on his ground-breaking teaching method; if you're a coach, this is a valuable resource to have in your book collection. Mr. Leonard was instrumental in the founding of ICF, which established industry standards, ethics, and credentialling for coaches. Sadly, Thomas Leonard passed away tragically at the young age of 49, but CoachU lives on and remains a leader in the life and performance coaching industry.

I started out helping people with the important issues in their lives, from stagnant careers and relationships to emotions and finances. Yes, I handled the gamut!

But starting a business is not an easy endeavor. In my previous jobs, I showed up to a stocked office with a desk, a pretty good chair, a phone, business cards, notepads, pens and pencils, and a plan for success. There was a company website, social media accounts, and a marketing campaign already in place. I was reimbursed for travel and any other expense I incurred while doing company business. Heck, I was even given awards for doing my job extremely well!

Entrepreneurs, however, are on our own. We have to buy a desk and a pretty good chair, and the minute we answer our newly set-up phone, we reach for the pen and pad of paper that isn't there. Why? Because we haven't thought of filling our office with all of the things we took for granted when we worked for a large corporation.

Did I mention we have to pay for it all?

> *"As an entrepreneur, it's up to you to educate yourself. It's up to you to learn speaking skills and people skills. It's up to you to try (and usually fail, but to try again) all sorts of ventures. The rest is a combination of hard work, being at the right place... at the right time... with the right thing...oh yes... and more (never ending) hard work."*
>
> **Gene Simmons**

And then there's the business and legal considerations, from contracts to company structure and insurance. Entrepreneurs have to pay for that, too, in more ways than one.

Once all those details are sorted, the focus turns to funding. If you're an entrepreneur, one of the biggest questions you'll have to ask yourself multiple times a day is how will your business stay afloat? I started by increasing traffic to my digital marketing platforms, and converting this traffic into sales. This, by the way, is much easier to accomplish on paper. Entrepreneurs are also responsible for procuring contact lists, employing people to call and email potential buyers, or simply hiring telemarketers to make the calls instead.

It sounds like I was fully prepared for entrepreneurship, doesn't it? Sadly, I was not. I was, however, completely overwhelmed and second-guessing my life decisions. I asked myself if having my own, independent business was still of paramount importance, and really worked on getting an accurate answer. Anything less than an effusive "YES!" meant that my heart wasn't into it, which would not benefit my future clients.

And my answer was that life coaching wasn't as fulfilling as I'd expected. Here I was, dealing with other people's emotions and complex life issues, when my own life issues were more than enough for me to handle. Too much for me to handle, if I'm being perfectly honest!

I'm not exaggerating when I tell you thoughts of whether I should continue coaching ran through my head at least a thousand times a day. Give or take.

Then came Buck, an enterprise sales leader who'd seen my CV on the Co-Active Coaching Institute's website. My success in the field piqued his interest, and we started meeting for coaching sessions related to his career. It all suddenly clicked; I found my passion.

It's an incredible feeling to be able to coach clients on improving their performance, moving up the sales leader board, and increasing their wealth. My Sales Navigation System really came in handy because it enabled my prospective clients to see the lucrative benefits of fewer surprises and greater certainty of a successful outcome.

(Note: If you're interested in raising your own performance levels, no matter your life's goals, I highly encourage you to read my book: *How to Become a $1 Million Enterprise Sales Leader*. It's an easy-to-follow road map to greatness available on bmcce.com.)

My clients learn the unique nuances of sales that elevate them from being a mid-level participant to a top-tier leader. I'm proud to tell you that many of my clients have closed millions of dollars in sales, and achieved the Top Sales Leader echelon in their organizations.

As a coach, I also work with entrepreneurs and founders as a volunteer for SCORE, a non-profit organization that's funded by the Small Business Administration and connects business mentors to small business. When they arrive at their first session, most don't have a plan in place for starting or improving their existing business. No matter how long they've been working on bettering their situation, nothing ever comes of their efforts. They've gotten stuck in a holding pattern.

There's a reason why a pattern is defined as a repeated design; it never changes itself.

> *"The most basic way to get someone's attention is this: Break a pattern."*
>
> **Chip Heath and Dan Heath**

They all needed a plan. That's precisely why I created a simple, intuitive tool anyone can use to Plan for Success (PFS). After a few qualifying questions, I ask the client if they have a business plan, marketing plan, or even a competitive plan. Ninety-five percent shake their head no. Very, very few have a plan, but it certainly isn't written down.

How does PFS work?

Step One: My client draws a circle and cuts it into several slices, like a pie.

Plan for Success Figure 1.

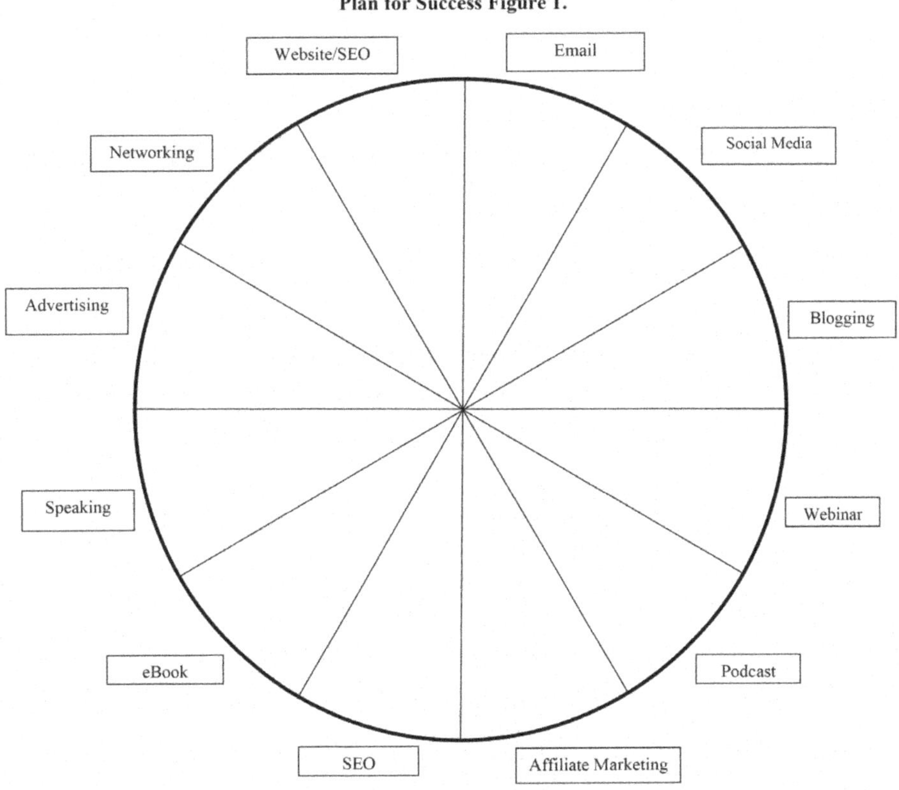

Step Two: Together, we brainstorm about marketing activities in which the client has engaged, from networking and public speaking to blogging and podcasting. We then give each of these pursuits a piece of the pie.

Step Three: Using a scale from zero to ten, I ask my client to rate their level of satisfaction in raising awareness about their business with each marketing tactic. My goal is for my client to determine which activity – or activities – will provide the biggest return on investment in the shortest amount of time and money spent.

Step Four: Let's proceed with a hypothetical client who chose *social media* first, but noted that their level of satisfaction is around a two out of ten. I'd ask them to create a number line, with zero at the far left, and ten at the far right, making a mark at the two. This gives clients a visual representation of where they are currently, and how much they need to improve.

Social Media (LinkedIn)

---

0 2 10

Step Five: It's time to create an Action Plan. First, my client and I brainstorm about how they'll improve their networking. Usually, their initial response is something along the lines of, "I...guess I'll join a few networking groups?" Yes, that's a good start, but we persist until they've identified as many *specific* ways as possible they can improve their social networking. Soon, the plan becomes theirs – not mine – and they are more likely to act on their commitments.

In this example, the client has created an Action Plan that includes:

- Research competitor's LinkedIn profiles and enhance my profile accordingly.
- Follow a couple of influencers in small business who can teach me how LI networking operates.
- Engage with influencers by commenting on their post.
- Start posting myself to create my LI community.
- Continue to comment on other influencer's post.
- Build LI network to more than 20,000 followers.
- Remember it's always better to give than receive.

Step Six: These goals won't happen on their own; it takes effort and a strict adherence to time parameters. I give most clients 60 days to effect the kind of change that will make a difference in their business.

Then I ask, "If you complete the Action Plan in 60 days, how satisfied will you be with your networking performance?"

Again, we make a new number line, moving the original satisfaction rate of two to their potential rating somewhere around five.

Social Media (LinkedIn)

____

0 5 10

"Won't that feel amazing?" I ask. "Now, what do you think that bump will look like in your business?"

They usually shrug, but they have a new glint in their eye. "My business ought to grow," they tell me.

Exactly.

When entrepreneurs take on too much, too soon, they get distracted. Unsurprisingly, this leads to a drop in discipline because "Oh, well. Nothing is working." The problem is that our brains are listening to these thoughts, and an overwhelming feeling of "This is never going to work!" takes over.

I regularly observe two reactions to this dejection. Sometimes, clients add more to their plan and think that's the answer, but some chuck it all to the wayside and consider their situation hopeless. It's frustrating, but I can see it coming from a mile away.

And that's exactly why I created PFS: to enable my clients to take ownership of their plans in manageable, tangible, accessible steps so that their optimism in themselves and their venture never wane. My goals are to organize their thoughts and narrow their focus, so their eye is always on the prize. When they leave my coaching session, they're hopeful because they have a workable plan, they're aware of their strengths and weaknesses, and they have written documentation of it all.

When I see them again, we review the plan and the client's goals, and talk about how they performed in their attempt to achieve them. At this point in our relationship, they've learned to be honest in their self-assessments, and are usually quite proud of their accomplishments. I am, too.

Depending on their individual goals, we will either stick to the same topic – networking, in this case – and perfect it, or move on to another slice in their marketing plan. It's a repeatable process that continues until my client has performed all the necessary steps in each activity to accomplish exactly what they set out to achieve.

It's a process to get from where you are to where you dream of being. But that's life, isn't it? If you have any doubts, just go back to the first page of my story.

Chapter Nineteen
Love, Actually

There are a few days in life that stick to your heart, and the 11th of August 2001 is one of those dates for me.

Five months earlier, I was meeting regularly with a therapist.

"My life is full," I told her. "But I'm lonely. I'm afraid I'll never meet the woman of my dreams."

"Your problem is that you *believe* you don't *deserve* to meet the woman of your dreams," she replied matter-of-factly.

Huh. Maybe she had a point.

I'd viewed myself as lacking my whole life. I knew the first time my grandmother shook her head and told me, "You are just like your father, Bill McCombs." that it was not a compliment, whatsoever. If I was just like him, I was the worst.

Plus, my expectations didn't align with my reality. If I was so mediocre – or worse! – then how in the world was I hoping to find an educated, intelligent, accomplished, well-traveled, and financially independent partner? I kept wishing for Miss America to come into my life, but if my therapist was right and I didn't believe I deserved Miss America, then I probably would miss her.

> *"If you think you can't make time to invest into your life at once now, you will be compelled to make time to count your regrets one by one later. By all means, you'll make time... So, make it now!"*
>
> **Israelmore Ayivor**

"Your soul mate hasn't materialized because you don't believe you have what it takes to meet your equal," My therapist continued. "That's why you keep settling for less."

It was time I worked on my self-esteem. No more repeating old patterns. It was high time I got out of my comfort zone.

I've already told you that my mother enrolled me and Patricia in dance lessons when we were young. Well, the reason it was so important to her was that dance gave her confidence and she hoped it would provide us with the same sense of personal satisfaction and pride.

"Dancing requires so many talents," she'd tell us over and over. "Agility, flexibility, and stamina, to name a few. It's also a nice way to socialize and meet other kids your age. And...dance builds confidence."

I fought it all the way because all I wanted to do was be outside with a ball in my hand, running and playing with my friends. But Mother won, and I took dance lessons for three long years.

After one of my therapy appointments, I serendipitously happened to see an advertisement for ballroom dance lessons. I instantly knew that finding someone who enjoyed dancing as much as I did could do the trick.

Back to August 11th, 2001. I'm in lower Manhattan at the ground level of the World Trade Center, taking part in a ballroom dance competition. The temperature outside was steaming around 105 degrees, but it got even hotter inside when I spotted the most gorgeous woman from across the room. She was effervescent in a purple ballgown, that she made, sprinkled with rhinestones, but her eyes sparkled even more vibrantly than her dress.

I couldn't help myself, and actually said out loud, "I sure would like to meet her."

That night, a group of us went to the 110th floor of the World Trade Center to have a drink and gaze out at the brightly lit landmarks scattered throughout the New York Harbor, including the always humbling Statue of Liberty. Exactly one month later, on September 11th, the exact spot where we'd enjoyed cocktails and conversation was gone for good, and the buildings in which we'd danced were utterly destroyed.

Time passed, and I continued taking dance lessons and meeting new people. I never could shake the vision of that woman from New York, though.

As luck would have it, I saw her again at a ballroom dance competition in Dallas. I attempted to flirt with her as we passed by one another on the dance floor, but she was playing hard-to-get. I considered it a win when she finally smiled at me and told me her name.

Pam. Now, my dream woman had a name.

We encountered each other once again in Columbus, Ohio at the largest dance competition in North America. This time, Pam showed a bit more interest in me. In a burst of confidence, I asked Pam for her email address; it felt less forward than asking for her phone number. She hesitated, then laughed, smiled, and promised to leave it on the hotel voice mail.

I was about to check out a few days later, and there was *still* no message from Pam. I'd grown up with the old adage "A watched pot never boils," but I could tell you a thing or two about a watched hotel phone! My heart raced, my palms got sweaty, and I'd lost almost all hope as I headed to breakfast. But when I returned to the room to pack up my bags, there it was: a blinking light indicating that someone had left a message.

It was Pam, telling me her email address. I wrote it down, listened to her message a few more times, and finally hung up the phone.

"Yes!" I exclaimed. There may have also been a fist pump in the air. Or two.

I let a week or so go by before I emailed Pam, but I didn't hear back for a solid month. A month. If you think it's challenging to watch a hotel phone and not lose your mind while waiting for a voicemail, imagine how many times I hit refresh on my inbox.

Shortly after the Christmas holidays, Pam finally returned my email. She had been at her sister's home in Montana for the holidays, and did not look at her email while she was there.

After a few months of exchanging messages and talking on the phone like high schoolers, we decided to reunite at a competition in Orange County near Pam's home. When we met, she was wearing a red sweater, jeans that fit her like a glove, sparkly heels, and a smile that lit up California.

I think I said something unforgettable. Like, "Hello."

Hey, I was nervous! My mouth felt like it was full of marbles, and I stumbled over most of my words.

It got better. Much better. We spent the entire Valentine's Day weekend competing in ballroom dancing against each other. After competing, we hung out at the bar having drinks with friends. Pam invited me to lunch at the famous Harbor Grill in Dana Point near her house, where – by the way – she picked up the check.

Afterwards, we drove up the road to Pam's house. At the bottom of the hill, just as we neared her driveway, the Pacific Ocean popped into full view.

Okay, living down the street from a vista like that is extremely impressive, I thought. And then I saw her home.

Standing in her foyer, looking south through her sweeping paned glass windows, was an even more incredible view of the ocean.

"Tea?" Pam offered.

"I'd love some tea," I replied.

I tried to play it cool, but inside I was thinking things like *This is the woman of my dreams* and *Don't blow it, Bruce* and *Boy, do I hate tea*. Still, I sipped on it like it was my favorite wine.

"I don't know if you're aware, but my dance partner is gay," Pam confessed. "He thought you were so cute! That's why I paid more attention to you at the Ohio competition."

"Were you intending on setting up the two of us?" I asked incredulously.

Pam giggled, and I fell in love for the fourth time that day. "I hadn't thought it all the way through!"

> *"your hand*
> *touching mine.*
> *this is how*
> *galaxies*
> *collide."*
>
> **Sanober Khan**

We laughed about that for a minute or two, and then she asked me if I'd like to see her middle son, Emo, play in his band at a local club. Wild horses couldn't tear me away from Pam, so I would've agreed to go anywhere at that moment – as long as we'd go together.

Just then, her sons Hazim and Emo bounded up the stairs and introduced themselves, along with Hazim's girlfriend, Celine. They were well-mannered and cordial, but in a hurry to get to the venue for Emo's performance.

Unbeknownst to me Pam's parents and extended family were going to attend the concert, too. They were an eclectic group who called themselves The United Nations because their ethnicities included Asians, Samoans, Latinos, Arabs, and Anglos.

I ended up next to her dad.

"I'm not a fan of the loud music," he said. "I prefer Tchaikovsky"

At least, that's what I think he said. The band was so loud, our conversation consisted of smiling and nodding at each other while mouthing words the other could not understand. When the performance ended, I exchanged pleasantries with him and Pam's stepmother, Maggie, and the rest of The United Nations. It was an unforgettable evening that only got better; we headed back to the dance competition to catch more dancing, and then consummated our spectacular weekend together.

On my flight home, I got lost in my thoughts. All of them were about Pam. I had honestly never met someone with whom I felt so comfortable. She was smart, funny, attractive, and well-traveled. She was also a wonderful dancer. She was so wonderful, in fact, that she usually won when we competed against each other!

Of course, the judges liked the women because they were beautiful and there were more of them than men. Hence, the women paid most of the dance floor fees so the judges wanted them to keep coming back to compete at different National Dance Council Association (NDCA) competitions throughout the year. At the time, NDCA was the governing body for professional and pro/am competitions throughout North America.

Pam and I met again a few weeks later, this time in Sedona, Arizona. She had never been, and I couldn't wait to see her experience that magical spot for the first time. Who knew what mystical outcomes we might experience together?

We'd been keeping in touch with regular calls and emails, and our relationship was progressing at a rapid pace. It was such a strange phenomenon to know exactly what another person is feeling, and share in their accomplishments, daily highs and lows, and delights...without the usual games played when two people start dating.

As soon as we met at the Phoenix airport, our connection electrified the air around us. Pam greeted me with her movie star smile, a passionate kiss, and a tight hug. A few of the other passengers in the airport whooped and clapped at our exuberance. Rather than be embarrassed, we smiled and waved.

I think we both realized what a gift it is to be loved.

> *"I was falling. Falling through time and space and stars and sky and everything in between. I fell for days and weeks and what felt like lifetime across lifetimes. I fell until I forgot I was falling."*
>
> **Jess Rothenberg**

We got our rental car and drove to the hotel where we were staying, the Phoenix Biltmore, designed by Frank Lloyd Wright. Ever since I visited the Guggenheim Museum in New York, I've been fascinated by his style of architecture. He was a visionary whose philosophy that a home should harmonize with the nature surrounding it changed architecture as we knew it. I liked his style.

As expected, the landscaping around the hotel was lush and green, and our room was beautifully furnished and overlooked the pool. We ate in the hotel restaurant that night, and the food was fine; good, not great, but I didn't care one bit about the food. Afterwards, I had a limo waiting to take us to a salsa club where we danced the night away. It wasn't a very happening place, but we were in our own little world anyway, giggling in the corner in between passionate dances.

That limo drive on the way to the club, however, was incredibly happening. So much so, that I wrote Pam a poem about it.

Limo Driving

After the meal we agreed on a deal
It was so cold outside, but we didn't scold
We jumped at the chance to ride in the stretch
I politely stared into her mystic eyes
For minutes until my passion consumed me

There was not much time to enjoy the ride
As Pam hopped in my lap where we tapped and rapped
More threads between us became known
I felt her soul in control, as we were limo driving

How could it be that we were meant to see
Because the driver knows the story goes
We are in love created from above
Always dreamed that we would be a team
We reached our destination where our passion was in formation
Salsa into the night till it's right
Our diver is a cowboy and listens to oldies
Make out break out no cares or worries
We reached the Biltmore at half past midnight with an erudite lady

As we were Limo Driving

The next morning, we drove north up Interstate 17, then turned left onto State 179 which is a direct route into Sedona. Pam sensed the magic as we passed the red rock formations including Bell Rock, the most photographed landmark in Sedona. I turned down the volume to Otmar Liebert, so we could take in the sights in silence. I'd seen it before, but it was breathtaking all over again as I watched Pam absorb her surroundings.

Our Bed & Breakfast was surrounded by red rock formations, conveniently located out our front door; hiking was only a few steps away. We put our baggage in the room, had a drink to relax, then hiked about a mile up the red rock. Nighttime came quickly, and dinner at one of the cheekiest restaurants in Sedona unfortunately did not live up to its reputation. Pam didn't care; she's never been into fine dining. Give her a peanut butter sandwich and chips, and she's a happy camper!

The next morning, we drove to Bell Rock and hiked almost to the top. Halfway down, we sat on the red rock, got quiet, and reflected on what we were feeling independently from each other.

Pam later told me that she married me while we sat quietly in meditation on Bell Rock.

Married me! *Me*!

Again, I tried to keep it cool. "Married me?" I asked.

"Yes," she beamed. "We're blessed because we have Divine Intelligence present in our love. You've given me more joy than I've ever felt before."

I had finally met my dream girl, my gift from heaven. This moment and this person were so worth the lifelong wait.

For the next two days, we hiked famous landmarks, drove through Oakville Canyon, lit a candle at a small unnamed chapel, had drinks at the Enchantment Resort, and ate burgers for dinner every day – Pam's choice, but I was happy to make her happy.

Always was, always will be.

Chapter Twenty
Head Over Heels

I think both Pam and I would agree that our lives began again when we met and fell in love, but I was also enjoying learning about her life before me.

Pam is half-Palestinian, and ended up marrying a Palestinian man. She'd spent the last 25 years of her life in Saudi Arabia and Jordan, raising their three boys while her husband worked and traveled throughout the Middle East.

I told her I loved hearing about her overseas life, and found it fascinating.

Pam shrugged, telling me, "My marriage and move across the world was honestly an escape from my stepmother. I couldn't live under the same roof with her any longer."

She moved back to Orange County after her divorce, happy to be close to her father again.

“He’s having some memory issues, you know...” she said.

I sighed, knowing exactly how she must be feeling. “A few years ago, I entered my mother in a brain research study at the Center for Brain Health. She’s been diagnosed with MCI, which stands for Mild Cognitive Impairment. I love the place; their mission is to slow the progression of dementia through social and cognitive activities. It’s fantastic.”

I think about our seemingly endless list of connections and similarities, and couldn’t help but believe that we were made for each other. She completed me with all the layers of her being.

I wouldn’t be able to see her again for six weeks. We planned to reunite for a Paul McCartney concert at Texas Stadium, and I couldn’t wait.

“If it’s okay with you, I’d love to invite my sister and her husband to the concert, too,” I mentioned. “She’s a big fan of McCartney.”

Pam was a Beatles fan, but not as interested in McCartney because she thought his music after the Beatles was a little dippy. I agreed up to a point, but I have always enjoyed McCartney as a songwriter.

“I can’t wait to meet them!” she replied enthusiastically.

We celebrated our time apart as a test of our commitment to each other. In the meantime, Pam and I lit up the airwaves by phone, text, and email while we were separated.

I learned so much about Pam in those six weeks, packed with conversations that continued over days, then weeks. I told her about my first trip to San Francisco, and she told me she, too, was inspired by the city.

“Haight Ashbury was my place,” she reminisced, telling me about the hippie movement and Summer of Love aesthetic. In the mid 1800s there was a banker named Haight, who got together with Ashbury, a member of the San Francisco Board of Supervisors, and planned the development for the area which included Golden Gate Park. Today it’s a blend of vintage clothing boutiques, record shops, bookstores, eclectic restaurants, and the infamous Filmore West.

"That's where I saw so many concerts," Pam said. "Janis Joplin, Jimi Hendrix..."

We talked about college, and I learned that she worked to pay for her education just like I did. She graduated from San Francisco State University with a degree in music.

> *"Every long separation is a test:*
> *A test to see how powerful or how weak*
> *the will of reuniting is!"*
>
> **Mehmet Murat Ildan**

Boy, those six weeks felt like a year. When I saw her again, a wave of calm blanketed me; together was the best state of being for us both. Our airport hellos were a thing of beauty, our passionate kisses and hugs always appreciated by those around us.

"I hope you like my place," I told her after packing up her suitcases in my car. For some odd reason, I was nervous about her reaction. I shouldn't have been, though; I was living in an 1800 sq. foot condo surrounded by big oak trees, hilly terrain, a creek nearby, tennis courts where *the* Martina Navratilova use to practice, and beautiful Stevens Park municipal golf course nearby. I recently had it remodeled, choosing Seafoam for the walls and Butter Yellow for the bathrooms, and they'd laid granite countertops in both the kitchen and bathrooms. I knew it looked sharp, but my old not-good-enough mindset filled me with insecurity.

My nerves stayed the whole car ride, tempered a bit by passing fields of bluebonnets in full bloom lining the highway.

"Those flowers are so beautiful!" Pam exclaimed.

"It's Texas' state flower," I told her. "The shape of bluebonnet petals looks like the bonnets women wore during the pioneer days to protect their face from the sun. Lady Bird Johnson's pet project as First Lady was highway beautification, and she kept it going after the White House."

I was happy for the bluebell distraction. It kept my mind from racing: Will she love my place as much as I do? Will we have as much fun as we did the last time we were together? Is our spark still as powerful?

I don't want to spoil the story, but the answer was yes to all.

Pam raved over my condo, loved my neighborhood, and wanted to see all of my favorite haunts. So, we had lunch at The Dancing Marlin, my favorite burger joint in Deep Ellum, owned by a Greek guy who loved dancing and deep sea fishing. The name of his restaurant was a no brainer! That burger is the best in Dallas: 90% sirloin beef with a perfect bun, toasted on the inside and a puffy crisp on the outside.

When we got back to my place, we chilled out by the pool in a bit of a food coma until it was time to get ready for the concert.

Patricia and Bill soon arrived. I was pleased at how easily my sister and Pam got along. Both Beatles' fans and both survivors of the hippie movement in the sixties, they chatted nonstop until we found our seats at the stadium. We had terrific view of the stage on the lower deck, but we still used binoculars to get a great view of the band. You could tell that Paul loved playing rock and roll even in his late fifties. He played several Beatles songs including *Back in the USSR* and *Yesterday*. He also played tunes from his Wings' albums and new music from his latest CD, *Driving Rain*. It was a night to remember forever.

They all were, though.

I took her to my favorite restaurant in Dallas – Nana Grill – located on the 22nd floor of the Anatole Hotel. Trammel Crowe, the world-famous real estate developer, built the Anatole and named it after his favorite restaurant in Copenhagen, Denmark. The restaurant overlooked downtown Dallas, but that view had nothing on mine. Pam and I tore up the dance floor to live music until the early hours of the morning!

I'd thought about asking Pam to marry me since our trip to Sedona, but we had only been dating for three months. It was too soon, right?

But then Pam asked, "Would you like to get married?"

I was flabbergasted. "W-W-WHAT?" I sputtered. "Not fair! I was going to ask you first!"

We had a big laugh and then dashed to the dance floor because our favorite Latin Cha Cha music was playing. After dancing for an hour or so, we sat back down, and the conversation got serious.

"I think we should be engaged a year," I suggested.

"Then that brings us to the first day of Spring," Pam nodded. "Let's do it."

Pam preferred a private, intimate wedding that included just the two of us.

"And then we could have a reception a few weeks after so that all our friends and family can meet and celebrate together."

I liked that idea a lot.

Pam met my mother and a few other family members the next day at The Dancing Marlin – Pam loved the burgers even more than I did! – and the two of them got along wonderfully. Midway through lunch, we told everyone the news. I watched my mother's reaction intently because she knew everything, including the tiresome journey I'd taken in my lifelong attempt to find my soulmate. Oh, the look on her face; she knew I found her.

> *"Maybe love at first sight isn't what we think it is. Maybe it's recognizing a soul we loved in a past life and falling in love with them again."*
>
> **Kamand Kojouri**

Just before Pam boarded the plane to take her back home, she told me she'd spend the next few weeks investigating Hawaiian wedding packages. I was so sad to see her go, but also excited about our future together. I wanted to announce it over the airport intercom: "I am getting married! She's my gift from God! I am the luckiest guy in the world!"

That would've been something.

We hugged and kissed goodbye even more passionately than before, which is saying a lot. I stood there while Pam handed her ticket to the flight attendant, and then – just like in the movies – she turned and waved, blowing me a kiss. I waved back, mouthing the words, "I love you!"

The next several months, Pam and I commuted back and forth from Dallas to Orange County, taking dance lessons with some of the top ballroom dance coaches in the USA. We were a Ten Dance couple, which meant we competed in the five International Ballroom (standard) dances – Waltz, Foxtrot, Tango, Quick Step, and Viennese Waltz – along with the five International Latin dances – Rumba, Samba, Paso Doble, Cha Cha, and Jive.

Ten Dance was extremely demanding, and required lots of practice, coaching and stamina. We were both competitive and wanted to be recognized as one of the top Ten Dance amateur couples in the country for our age group.

On one of my many trips to see Pam, we were out to dinner with her dad and stepmother. While Pam and Maggie were deep in their own conversation, I asked Bob for Pam's hand in marriage.

"Of course, son," he said. "But treat her right!" He was concerned because her last marriage ended badly, and he did not want to see Pam hurt again.

I informed him that we were working out any potential obstacles in our relationship during our engagement. "Once we're married," I assured him. "It's until death do us part!"

He truly liked that, and I truly liked him.

Bob was quite a character. Born in Haifa, Palestine, the youngest of eight children, he and his family immigrated to the United States before World War II. They settled in the San Francisco area where he went to school until he joined the Army to fight in the war. Since he spoke Arabic, he turned his bilingual talent into an asset and became a translator. If you were ever seated next to him at a dinner party, you'd be lucky. He had some amazing tales.

After the war, Bob attended UC Berkley, earned a degree in civil engineering, and got married. He and his wife soon had three daughters: Pam, Nancy, and then Kathy.

Unfortunately, Pam's parents divorced when she was very young, and all three girls unanimously decided to live with their father. Eerily similar to how I felt about my father growing up, Pam believed that her mother abandoned her and her sisters. As a result, the relationship with their mother became estranged. Bob remarried, but Pam did not get along with June, her new stepmother, because she tried to be the disciplinarian when her dad was out of town on business.

Bob designed highways and bridges for the State of California. After a few years, he moved from the public sector and went to work for The Irvine Company, a large real estate developer based in Orange County, California. Bob was instrumental in designing shopping centers and residential and commercial developments.

Bob loved to gamble, and he and June were regulars in Vegas. During one of their trips, June collapsed in the lobby of the Caesar's Hotel. They hurried her into an ambulance and whisked her to the hospital. June went into a coma, and died four months later. Fortunately, Pam and June had made up before this tragedy happened.

A few years after June's death, Bob started dating Maggie, a woman he met at The Irvine Company. Maggie was born in Wales, and eventually moved to London. Prior to her position at The Irvine Company, Maggie worked in the airline industry, which fed her love of travel. Together, she and Bob got married and traveled the world, and Maggie quickly became a respected matriarch in Pam's family.

I felt lucky to know them, and even luckier that I would someday soon be able to call them family.

After receiving Bob's blessing that I could marry Pam, I started on a hunt for the perfect wedding ring. If I wasn't coaching my clients or helping my mom at the Center for Brain Health, you could find me looking at diamonds at a jewelry store. I must have shopped at five different stores before I found the one: a radiant two-carat diamond ring at Bachendorf's luxury jewelry store.

Radiant cuts appear bigger because of the cut corners and flat pavilion, which is the lower part of the gemstone. (See? I told you I spent a lot of time with diamonds!) That means a two-carat radiant will look larger than most other diamond cuts. Another important point is that a radiant cut uses a larger percentage of the original diamond, so very little goes to waste. The color and clarity were at the top end of their range in quality as well.

Pam found a wedding planner on Maui that she liked, especially when she learned that they offered a walking labyrinth on a private beachfront. We agreed that we would be the only attendees, with the exception of Eve, our minister.

"March 21st?" Pam clarified.

"March 21st," I agreed. The first day of Spring. The time when the natural world revives and reinvigorates after a cold winter, when flowers bloom and birds lay eggs and hope abounds. What a perfect day to celebrate our love.

> *"Every day is brightly colored like Spring when you meet the right person in life!"*
>
> **Luffina Lourderaj**

I booked an oceanfront room at the Four Seasons, and first class seats on American Airlines. The day of our flight, I first flew to Los Angeles and rendezvoused with Pam at LAX. By now, you know that airport Pam was a really sexy Pam. But this time, she was somehow even sexier. Maybe it was her black and white polka dotted dress, maybe it was the way she'd styled her hair that day, or maybe it was the realization that this woman was going to be my wife.

We drank champagne during the flight – enough, but not too much – and talked about our new life together until we got to our hotel.

"I'm sorry, but your room isn't ready just yet," we were told, so we took in the sights of the gorgeous, open lobby, people-watching and breathing in the ocean air until the concierge came to collect us.

Our room was worth the wait.

The first thing we saw upon entering was the vibrant array of indigenous flowers I'd ordered, along with a bottle of Dom Perignon on ice. The sky was Maui blue, blending at the horizon into the water, and I was so pleased Pam had chosen this idyllic island for our beginning.

But I was getting a little nervous. In two short days, we were getting married.

We filled them with dinners and dancing, a trek to the Haleakalā volcano crater, an afternoon of scuba, and more dancing.

On March 21st, we woke up a little late to the sound of a howling wind. The leaves on the palm trees flew in our direction, and the ocean overflowed with white caps. You didn't have to be a mystic to believe a shake-up was on its way to us.

> *"And forget not that the earth delights to feel your bare feet and the winds long to play with your hair."*
>
> **Khalil Gibran**

When we arrived at the wedding venue, we were both overwhelmed by the beauty around us. We walked around the back of the house to see the labyrinth, a white walking trail outlined in purple blooms covered the grass.

At the end of it, I thought, *is where my life changes*. I couldn't wait.

Eve, our minister, told us that the labyrinth symbolized our individual life journeys before this day. As we made our way to the place we'd exchange our vows, it felt like I was walking toward the greatest change in my life to date. It was me and Pam, Eve, and one very interested black cat, watching intently from five feet away.

"When you walk back through the labyrinth, together this time, your journey will forevermore continue on the same path," Eve said.

I looked at my soon-to-be-wife, stunning in a white dress she'd made herself, her veil sailing straight out behind her, hoisted by the literal winds of change, and all I could think was, *I made it. I've worked hard on myself, acknowledged my strengths and weaknesses, and changed my patterns to become the man I've always hoped to be.*

It was all worth it.

Chapter Twenty-One
A Very Full Dance Card

Our first amateur competition as a married couple would take place at the Ohio Star Ball. We had both competed there before with our Pro/Am partners, and it's where I'd asked for Pam's email address, so it kind of felt like we were coming home, in a way.

The Ohio Star Ball (OSB) grew from a relatively small studio competition in the 1970s to become the largest ballroom dance festival in North America. Sam, the charismatic founder of the event, has been a pioneer growing DanceSport for the last 50 years. He was instrumental in getting OSB televised on the Public Broadcasting Service, emceed by Mitzi Gaynor in the 1990s, and it became the highest rated show on PBS at the time.

He has always impressed me as the ultimate connector. In fact, one of Sam's catch phrases is, "There are no strangers at the Ohio Star Ball – just people we have not met!"

Pam and I performed well in Ohio, coming in second place in Cha Cha and Rumba, and third in Samba.

"Pretty good, considering we just started dancing together!" I told Pam.

OSB was a great opportunity to prepare for our first amateur competition in Houston, Texas. USA Dance is the national governing body for amateur DanceSport in the United States, recognized as such by the World DanceSport Federation (WDSF), which USA Dance is a member of, the US Olympic Committee (USOC), and the Amateur Sports Act of the United States Congress. The nonprofit was founded by Normand Martin, a leading social and competitive ballroom dance champion in 1965. Normand organized a group of interested dancers who created bylaws to guide the new amateur dance organization.

USA Dance organizes regional competitions around the country, and also hosts the annual National DanceSport Championships each year, which awards titles and the opportunity to represent the US at the World Championships normally held in Europe. The organization has thousands of paying members and over 100 chapters across the USA, while WDSF has 92 member countries.

The Houston chapter organized the national qualifying event (NQE) where we would compete, hosted at a local college. By placing in the top three in either Ballroom or Latin, we could earn points to qualify for the National Championships.

About three months prior to the Houston competition, Pam and I learned new routines for Waltz and Quick Step. Normally there are two to 12 competitors on the dance floor at the same time, but now it was just me and Pam and around 200 spectators staring at us. We were accustomed to an audience...just not our very own audience!

We got through the Waltz with no problems. Halfway through our Quick Step, however, we forgot our routine. And we didn't forget just once. We didn't even misstep twice. No, we stopped on the floor three, interminable times.

I was so stressed, but I was trying to contain my emotions.

"Can you stop squeezing my hand so tightly?" Pam murmured in my ear.

Oops. I guess I wasn't containing them as well as I thought.

> *"Dance, when you're broken open. Dance, if you've torn the bandage off. Dance in the middle of the fighting. Dance in your blood. Dance when you're perfectly free."*
>
> **Rumi**

Later, when the emcee announced the award for our dance over the sound system, he said, "In heat number 21, number 341, second place goes to Bruce and Pamela McCombs."

Second place wouldn't have been bad under normal circumstances, but no one else competed against us! Some new friends we had met earlier in the day came up to us to offer some comfort.

"No worries," the wife said. "In our first competition, I experienced a major wardrobe malfunction; the straps on my dress came loose and I flashed my chest to over 600 people!"

We laughed and laughed because misery sure loves company.

And then the husband leans in and says, "She came in first place!"

It was a great feeling to meet new friends and have a ball together, even more so knowing they had danced in our shoes in one way or the other.

We quickly ran to change into our Latin costumes because we were competing in the Senior division with three other couples. One of the couples won the Senior Latin National Championship eight months earlier, so we knew the competition would be stiff. Pam and I were both dressed in black, which is a common color in DanceSport, with little skin showing because USA Dance's dress code was much stricter than when we competed in Pro/Am competitions.

We competed five Latin dances to compete in back-to-back: Cha Cha, Samba, Rumba, Jive, and Paso Doble. This time we did not forget any of our routines, completing each one without missing a step. (Or, at least, without missing a noticeable step!)

"In heat 52, number 341," the emcee announced over the loudspeaker. "First place goes to Bruce and Pamela McCombs!"

What? Pam and I looked at each other, both visibly shocked. Then we looked at our competitors' faces, and we knew we hadn't imagined the announcement. They appeared even more perplexed that we were, wondering how this could have happened. Still, they were gracious and congratulated us with class.

We won. We had just beat the reigning Senior Latin Champions. From second place in Ballroom when no competitors were on the floor, to first place in Latin. Pam and I beamed ear to ear as everyone surrounded us with congratulations.

I tried to feel worthy of the award, but there was always that piece of my brain that whispered, "You don't deserve this. You've never been good enough, and that hasn't changed." I did my best to ignore it, but I told myself that we won because of Pam or that we won because the judges wanted a shake-up. I thought of anything and everything that could justify my (surely) accidental success.

But seven months later, we competed in Las Vegas at the Holiday Classic, two weeks before Christmas, and we beat the Latin National Champions again!

Huh.

A month later, we flew to New York to compete in the Manhattan Amateur Championships (MAC), held at Columbia University. We stayed at the Pierre Hotel, across from Central Park and the Plaza Hotel, so that we could be close to the performance venue.

It was freezing in New York that January, snowing and a positively bone chilling five degrees. But we'd chosen this competition because it drew the best competitors in the country in all divisions. We'd done our homework, too, scouring the USA Dance website to review the score-sheets of our competitors, seeing how they placed in other competitions. Two of the Latin couples were consistently either number one or two in NQEs in the Senior division.

Our first dance, Pam drew everyone's attention in a purple and black Latin dress covered with light-catching rhinestones. I was a good complement to her in a white button-down shirt and black Latin pants. The floor was crowded with competitors, but we lined up right in front of the judges and made sure there was no obstruction of their view.

It turned out to be a great strategy.

"First place," the emcee announced. "Goes to Bruce and Pamela McCombs!"

This time, our competitors didn't try to hide their looks of utter disgust at losing to newbies. I get it; we were on their turf, in their city, and we beat them. Still, empathy aside, we were elated.

> *"It is deeply satisfying to win a prize in front of a lot of people."*
>
> **E.B. White**

It was late when we got back to the Pierre Hotel, and the only other two people in the lobby happened to be Bill and Melinda Gates.

"You're very happy!" they both noticed. "You must've had a great night?"

"We sure did!" we beamed. "We just won a dance competition!"

When we got back to the room, we opened a bottle of Johnny Walker Black and relived each of the five dances in which we'd competed.

We were on a roll. Four months later, we won the Senior Latin division at the Emerald Star Ball in Los Angeles, and then we returned to New York to dance at the Manhattan Dance Championship, defeating one of the couples we'd bested a few months earlier.

If our competitors' looks could kill, we'd be dead.

We continued to have success at the Snow Ball Classic in Vancouver, the USA Dance National Championships, and many other events across the country.

During one of our dance weekends, I forgot to pack my Latin dance pants.

"I'm sure I can just buy a pair from one of the vendors," I said to Pam, not really worried. They were just pants. How difficult would it be to find pants?

Well, I found pants, but I could not find pants to fit. The pair I bought was way too long, and we couldn't find a needle and thread to hem them properly. Our solution was to simply cut off the excess from the legs, and hem them with safety pins.

We got through Cha Cha with no problem from my pants, but a couple of the safety pins popped loose part way through our Samba. By the time we got to our fourth dance, which was Jive, most of the safety pins had come undone and my pant legs were now covering my shoes. Not only was it not a good look, but it made dancing quite hazardous as the loose material got between my shoes and the dance floor. It all made the floor very slippery. I felt like I was skating on very thin ice!

We're sunk, I thought. How can we win Jive if half my kicks and flicks are obscured by these crazy pant legs? Added to the stress was the fact that there were 3-400 spectators watching me do my best not to slide off the dance floor.

Despite my wardrobe malfunction, we won. One of the judges was from Australia, and he had a good chuckle when he handed us our award. "Hey mate," he smiled. "I guess you forgot your pants?"

It was time to reassess our successes and flops in dance, and we came to the realization that we should stop expending our extra attention and energy on Ballroom when we were crushing it in Latin. We told our Ballroom coaches about our decision, and they couldn't help but agree with us. With the reduction in dances from ten to five, we also experienced a drastic reduction in stress!

Now, we could turn all our attention to Latin, focusing on Cha Cha, Samba, Rumba, Paso Doble, and Jive. We had a soft spot for them all.

The Cha Cha originated in Cuba, and evolved out of the Cuban Triple Mambo for its one-two-three quick steps. In fact, it was originally called the Cha Cha Cha because that's the sound that the dancers' shoes made as they performed the dance. The dance involves minimal movement of the upper torso, while the hips, legs, and feet do all the work.

Samba originated on the Brazilian plantations where the African rhythms of slaves fused with European music, gradually making its way to the slums of Rio de Janeiro. It's so interesting to me that what began from a persecuted culture evolved into the symbol of a country! Samba is now the national dance of Brazil, celebrated every year during carnival where hundreds of thousands of people dress up in costumes and dance through the streets. We became acquainted with it in the US in the late 1920s with Fred Astaire and Dolores del Rio's film *Flying Down to Rio*. Samba eventually turned into a couples' dance in Ballroom Dance competitions in 1956.

The first Rumba competition took place in the Savoy Ballroom in 1930. Five years later, George Raft appeared with Carole Lombard in a movie called *Rumba*, in which he played a suave dancer who won the lady through dancing. Rumba captured the imaginations of ballroom dance enthusiasts immediately. It's not surprising that rumba is used as a synonym for party in northern Cuba.

Paso Doble means two steps, and is my absolute favorite dance of them all. The dance came from a 1930s French military march under the name Paso Redoble, but also has some Spanish roots, as well. The dance resembles the nature of the bullfight, so stern looks on the faces of competitors and its staccato steps are hallmarks of the dance. Paso, as the dance is often referred to, was introduced as a competitive Ballroom Dance in the 1950s.

Jive was first demonstrated in 1934 by Cab Calloway, a popular singer, dancer, and musician of our time. It really caught on in the US in the 1940s, heavily influenced by the African/American Swing and Lindyhop. Depending on who you ask, the name either originated from jive being a form of glib talk, or from African dance terms. This is a high tempo form of East Coast Swing that features a beat of one-ah-two, three-ah-four, five-ah-six, a rock step, and a bunch of kicks and flicks. Oddly, Jive is one of the most criticized dances; ballroom dancing guru Alex Moore once said he had never seen anything uglier.

But then, he never saw me and Pam dance the steps.

Each of these dance styles sounds hard enough on their own, but competitive Latin ballroom dancers must have tremendous stamina to compete at the championship level because all five dances are performed back-to-back with around ten second breaks in between each dance.

After five years of dancing together, Pam could barely walk because she had severe arthritis in both of her hips. Previously, she owned a fitness club overseas where she taught aerobics, living in the moment of youth, not considering the later effects of such high-impact exercise on her aging body. Pam eventually had two hip replacements, three months apart. Her rehabilitation lasted six months, during which time we didn't even attempt to think of anything dance-related.

> *"Injuries are our best teachers."*
>
> **Scott Jurek**

By the time we started dancing again, we were rusty, and our movements were slow. Our first competition at the MAC in New York brought us face-to-face with our two formidable competitor couples, and this time we came in third place. We were disappointed, but our results meant we had to work harder to get our speed back to achieve competitive sharpness.

Ultimately, we returned to form and won our next Latin title at the prestigious Gumbo Classic in Baton Rouge, Louisiana, against top competitors. We poured our heart and soul into our practices, videotaped them to correct our technique, and corrected most – if not all – of our flaws. Our hard work paid off because we won all five Latin dances in our next competition in Las Vegas.

I'm so grateful to medical science. After two hip replacements, Pam was able to return to top form within 18 months. Pam loved to dance more than anything, from the competition aspect to making her own gorgeous costumes and dressing up in them.

We competed in the Desert DanceSport Classic held in the Palm Springs area for several years. The California desert has 350 days of sunshine a year, with an average rainfall of five inches annually, and its hottest month is July when temperatures soar up to 120 degrees.

So guess when they held the Desert DanceSport Classic? If you guessed the middle of July, you are correct.

Despite the heat, the competition always enjoys a high attendance rate because it is held at the Marriot Hotel, which has an outstanding reputation, a terrific ballroom in which to dance and spectate, an energetic pool scene, and many top golf courses nearby.

A few days before the competition one year, I experienced pain in my left thigh, just above the knee. Whenever I moved, pain radiated up to my hip. Unfortunately, dance requires a bit of movement!

I saw an orthopedic specialist who convinced me to get a cortisone shot to take away the pain, but it offered no relief whatsoever. I broke the news to Pam that we had to cancel the competition and stop dancing until I got the pain under control. It was a huge disappointment for the both of us, especially since we'd only just returned to competitive dancing form after Pam's hip replacements.

I was hopeful that this would be a quick fix, and I'd be back to the dance floor in no time at all.

Chapter Twenty-Two
In Sickness and In Health

In all, Pam and I won 11 Senior Latin championships at competitions across North America. We felt vibrant and alive and aware of the opportunities ahead of us, like we were living out the expression "The world is our oyster." Our days overflowed with dancing, meeting new friends while enjoying our old acquaintances, and competing. We lived and loved life to the fullest.

We traveled back and forth from Dallas to Orange County regularly, feeling equally at home in both places. We also moved from my bachelor pad in Kessler Park to a condo in Uptown, which was little north of downtown Dallas and right in the middle of all the action. We could walk to the American Airlines Center to watch sporting events and concerts, and attend galas like the annual New Year's Eve party. We enjoyed getting to know the restaurants and bars nearby, and became fixtures in The Arts District, from the Meyerson Symphony Center, Winspear Opera House, and Performance Hall to The Dallas Museum of Art.

I felt like we were on top of the world, which worried me. You know the saying: All good things come to an end.

It wasn't all rainbows and pony rides, though. As I mentioned, we enrolled my mother at The Center for Brain Health, which was part of the University of Texas at Dallas' School of Behavioral and Brain Sciences. Founded by Dr. Sandra Bond Chapman in 1999, CBH was a research institute focused exclusively on dementia and Alzheimer's.

In 1906, Dr. Alois Alzheimer noticed changes in the brain tissue of a woman who had died of an unusual mental illness. Her symptoms included memory loss, language problems, and unpredictable behavior. Beyond Dr. Alzheimer's research, however, no one really paid attention to this disease. The general assumption was that people get old and die, and memory loss was an expected side-effect.

My mom had mild cognitive impairment (MCI), so her decline wasn't obvious to those who weren't around her every day. Her memory and recall were good, but she did slur her words occasionally, and that's what caused me to enter her into the CBH program in the first place.

My grandmother slurred her words a few years before she died at the age of 95 with what we believe was Alzheimer's. Back then, there was hardly any research on dementia, so any reduction in capabilities was simply brushed off as senility or a normal symptom of old age. But since we learned with my grandmother that slurring was an indicator of a decrease in cognitive function, we were aggressively proactive trying to slow its progress in Mom.

CBH, where my mother was participating in Alzheimer's research, hoped their findings would definitively answer the question, "Does cognitive and social activity slow the progress of Alzheimer's?" Dr. Sandy, as we called her, recruited participants over the age of 65 who had been diagnosed with some form of dementia. Caregivers were required to be present during the testing by trained, licensed CBH scientist and researchers. We met once a week for two hours each time, which was physically and mentally draining for Mom, and emotionally draining for us.

It was an impressive program. They tested Mom on activities she enjoyed, like arranging the pictures from her numerous trips around the world in chronological order, or baking a cake from a recipe. She impressed us so very much at every single appointment with her work ethic and instinct to perform beyond the therapists' expectations, but her memory got the best of her within a year.

> *"Please remember the real me*
> *when I cannot remember you."*
>
> **Mountain Wisdom**

It was heartbreaking. Here was this giant in banking, a trendsetter for women, who raised three children as a single mom. An alum of The University of Texas who got a job as a teller, and was progressively promoted until she became the first female Vice President at the largest bank in Dallas. She spent 46 years at the same bank where she'd started her career, and earned and saved enough to become a millionaire. She'd traveled the world, and had more on her bucket list. So much more.

She'd lived a life full of accomplishments, and *now* her cognition was fading when she was supposed to be enjoying the fruits of her labor?

It felt so unfair.

A few days after the CBH study ended, Mom told my sister, "I know I'm not as sharp as I used to be."

When I heard that, it broke my heart and I tried to fight back the tears.

The dementia continued to steal my mother's memories faster than we could keep up. We entered her into an assisted living facility that had stellar reviews from families like ours. It also had a wonderful memory care unit when the time came that Mom could not care for herself. The location was ideal, right off Interstate 75 that cut right through the heart of Dallas, which made it convenient for both Patricia and me to visit.

The facility made sure my mom's dance card was always full with dozens of activities that kept her socially and cognitively active, but she just wasn't happy. Worse, she was starting to get depressed about her new way of life. We had to come up with a different idea, so we started brainstorming.

"I wish she could just move in with me," Patricia sighed.

I tilted my head and thought about what she'd just said. "What if we used some of Mom's money to invest in a bigger, more accessible home?" I wondered aloud. "We could hire full-time help so the caretaking burden wouldn't be entirely on you, and..."

"Mom would love that," Patricia interrupted. "And so would I."

So, that's exactly what we did.

The house was situated on an acre of land, with a beautiful swimming pool, sauna, whirlpool, and guest house. With these amenities literally in her backyard, Patricia was able to easily continue the social and cognitive activities in which Mom had participated at the Center for Brain Health. The water aerobics group my mother had joined when she retired was also close to Patricia's new home, which made the adjustment even easier.

It all fell into place so seamlessly, and we were optimistic that she'd feel more fulfilled and happier.

Patricia also made sure that Mom was able to continue her volunteer work at her favorite charities, including the Volunteer Nurses Association and a church that also taught arts and crafts, donating their wares to sell at fundraisers. Mom really enjoyed developing her artistic side while volunteering. When she was young, she never thought of herself as creative. Whether that thought was drilled into her by her own mother or teachers or friends, it stuck. By the time she became a single mother and worked full-time, she didn't have time for arts and crafts. It really moved me to finally see my mother enjoy herself.

Patricia even found her a job! Even though my mother had retired, it was in her DNA to equate living fully with working. She became a greeter at Walmart, three days a week for two hours a day, which was more than enough. I realized what a full-circle moment this was for my mother when I recalled a childhood story that we'd heard through the years.

"Grandaddy worked for the Katy Railroad," she'd tell us. "So we lived really close to a railroad when I was young. Every time a train passed, I'd wave at the people as it chugged by. I always loved it when they waved back."

My mother likely didn't remember that long ago memory, but we hoped it would bring back some unconscious warmth.

We found an excellent caregiver named Darby, who really became instrumental in my mother's well-being. She helped with every aspect of daily life – bathing, dressing, applying make-up, eating – until her assistance was completely necessary for my mom to function.

One day, Mom fell at Walmart. Fortunately, Darby was there to make a scary situation a little less frightening. Walmart management called an ambulance, and she was taken to a nearby hospital with hip complications. She'd had hip replacement surgery 15 years earlier, and it was time for her to have revision surgery anyway. This accident made it more of an urgent issue. Such a big surgery with an even more monumental rehabilitation period would've been hard on anyone her age, but adding her memory loss to it made it near impossible to recover. She was now 100% dependent on Darby, Patricia, and me.

> *"To care for those who once cared for us*
> *is one of the highest honors."*
>
> **Tia Walker**

While all this was happening, I was also focused on healing myself. My thigh injury still had me sidelined from dancing, which caused me great distress.

"My mom's Alzheimer's is upsetting enough," I confided to Pam. "But I've had dance as my outlet for the last few years to counterbalance it all."

At my annual physical, my blood pressure was elevated. The only other time I'd experienced that was at my military draft physical!

"Are you anxious about anything?" My doctor asked.

Well, let's see.

"I recently retired, and I'm still adjusting to not working. I'm a competitive dancer, but I haven't been able to compete because of an injury," I listed off my stressors one by one. "Oh, and my mother's dementia, which was already progressing at an upsetting rate, just went into overdrive after her recent hip surgery."

The doctor looked at me, nodded, and said, "That certainly can cause anxiety, but it should subside if you exercise, get eight hours of sleep, and relax. Come back in a month, and I'm sure we'll see some improvement."

Could it be that easy? I thought.

(Spoiler alert: It was not that easy.)

A couple of weeks later, I had my regular dental exam.

"Hmmm," my dentist said.

"Ahhh?" I asked while her instrument was still in my mouth.

"There's a small white lesion on your tongue," she noted. "Given the look and feel of it, I want you to have it checked by a periodontist."

"Is it serious?!" I was instantly worried.

"Relax, Mr. McCombs! I like to err on the side of overly cautious. Let's check it out to be sure it's not cancer, okay?"

Her concern really put me on edge. Cancer?! On top of everything else?! I couldn't catch a break.

That eight hours of sleep my GP recommended was out the window. For the next few days, I walked around like a zombie. My ears were suddenly plugged, and I experienced random bouts of vertigo.

I put off scheduling an appointment with a periodontist because I was seeing my regular doctor in a few days to check up on my anxiety. Boy, was he going to be unhappy with my progress with sleeping and relaxing!

I told him all about what the dentist said, clearly in a panic.

He looked at it carefully, and then calmly said, "I doubt that's cancer. But let's follow-up with a periodontist to be sure."

My heart rate slowed a little.

"As for your ears," he continued. "You have a severe allergy and it's plugging them up, which is also why you have vertigo. I'm going to write you a prescription, and it should all be resolved quickly."

His calm confidence had an effect on my stress levels, but I wouldn't be able to sleep until I figured out for sure if this lesion was cancerous or not. From the time I woke up in the morning until I finally fell asleep, and through all the fitful wake-ups in between, I obsessed over this lesion.

"Please don't be there," I'd mutter every time I checked on it in the mirror. And every time, I was disappointed and more stressed, if that was possible.

The periodontist told me that the only way to find out if the lesion was cancerous was to biopsy it, but that she wanted to wait a few weeks to see if the lesion would go away on its own.

"Can you wait just a few more weeks?" she smiled, knowing I was stressed.

"No problem," I smiled back.

I was lying. There was a problem, and it was this lesion, and I wouldn't be able to stop worrying about it until I knew whether or not it was worrisome!

"I just need to go to the gym and work out," I told Pam. "I need to be physically exhausted so that I'm too tired to even think about this lesion!"

So there I was, at the gym, completing a sitting bench press set. I guess I let the weights come back too far, and heard a pop in my chest. It wasn't accompanied by pain, so I didn't think much of it and went about the rest of my day.

I spent the afternoon at my sister's house so I could help with my mother. Pam was away in Orange County on jury duty, so it was just me and my mom and sister for the day. I hopped in the pool, and thought *Now this is good. No more stress, Bruce. You got it?*

"Bruce?" Patricia peered closely at my chest. "What's that bump sticking out?"

I looked down at it, and couldn't believe what I saw.

"You have GOT to be kidding!"

A few days later, I tried to take a quick power nap, and began to feel shortness of breath. It got so serious that I went to the emergency room. After a few scary moments ruling out a heart attack, they diagnosed me with costochondritis which is an inflammation of the cartilage that connects the ribs to the sternum. I was given ibuprofen, and sent home.

If I thought I was low on sleep before this latest injury, I was in for a rude awakening. No pun intended; I was already awake, and had been for over a month.

I was completely on edge. My thoughts raced out of control. They went something like this: I have a white spot on my tongue that might be cancerous, excruciating pain in my thigh, and my mother is losing her cognition. I can't dance, I can't work out, I can't even sit at my computer to get work done, and my wife has to drive me everywhere because it's too painful to turn the steering wheel. I exaggerated all the what-ifs, convincing myself that I was going to lose my tongue, I'd be immobilized for the rest of my life, I'd go broke from not working, and my mother will die from Alzheimer's yesterday.

I finally called my GP and said, " Doctor, I'm completely on edge. So much so, that I'm having horrible thoughts."

"Describe the thoughts," he said.

I hesitated, then chose complete honesty in the moment. "I feel like I can't keep living like this."

It was a Wednesday, the day before Thanksgiving. Everyone seemed to be out of the office, preparing for the holiday, but my doctor replied with urgency in his voice.

"I'm going to try my best to get you in to see one of my colleagues. Stay by the phone."

Five minutes later, he called back and said, "You have an appointment to see a psychiatrist at four o'clock."

I told Pam that I had an appointment, and she was happy to drive me. I'm sure I was driving her crazy with my own craziness. But she remained calm, loving, and understanding while I struggled.

"Something is happening with you, and we just have to fix it. That's all." She reassured me the entire drive to the appointment. "You're going to be fine. I promise."

Dr. Stein's waiting room was so tiny, it made me instantly claustrophobic. I tapped my foot nervously, and tugged on my sweater. It felt like I was covered in bugs, and they were biting me ferociously.

Boy, was I a mess.

Then the doctor opened the door with a big smile, introduced himself, and invited us into his office. Dr. Stein was short, a little overweight, with a beard and glasses. He told us he knew my doctor from when they interned together at a hospital in Boston many years ago. While he talked, my eyes wandered to the bookshelf behind him, stacked with medical books.

He offered us something to drink, but we declined. I wanted to get on with it. I was nervous, filled with anxiety and curiosity, and I couldn't wait to find a solution for how I was feeling. I wanted the pain and perpetual sense of unease to be over.

"Okay," he clasped his hands together on top of the desk and leaned toward us. "What brings you here today?"

"Thank you for seeing us on such short notice," I said. "And just before Thanksgiving. I'm sure you have a lot on your schedule."

And then I told him everything, from my mother's condition for the past nine years, my dance injury and costochondritis that had all but incapacitated me, to the white spot on my tongue. "I had it biopsied, and the results came back as dysplasia. Abnormal cells. Possibility of them someday turning into cancer. Sorry if I'm telling you things you already know. Anyway, I need to have it removed before Christmas, and I'm really worried about that. I'm worried about it all."

Dr. Stein nodded, and asked, "What are you feeling right now?"

"Well," I replied. "Nothing good. I feel like I'm about to shatter every time I move an inch, like I'm a pane of glass that's just been smashed with a baseball. Every symptom I experience gets magnified in my mind until I'm sure I'm going to die."

I shook my head, embarrassed to say the next part.

"I called my GP because I had weird thoughts about my life that I've never felt before. If this is how I'm to live, I don't want to live anymore."

Dr. Stein had heard enough. "Listen. You're experiencing many stressors simultaneously, and something chemically in your body has been altered and come off the tracks. I think you've got depression and an anxiety disorder, but the good news is that I can prescribe you some meds to help."

He wrote out a prescription and handed it to me, and I grabbed it like it was a life preserver thrown to me in the middle of the ocean.

"I wont get addicted to these meds, will I?" I asked.

"Let's try them and see how you respond," he answered. "They should definitely help you get some sleep."

We drove back home after the Walgreens' pharmacist filled my prescription, and I hesitantly swallowed one of the pills. Within ten minutes, I felt relaxed for the first time in months.

Pam looked at me and could instantly tell that a weight had been lifted from my shoulders. "Okay," she smiled. "We've got this."

It wasn't one and done, though. I woke up the next morning to my same old feelings, and they only disappeared when I took more pills.

"I hated how I felt before," I said to Pam. "But I hate this dependence on medicine, too."

"Let's just get through the next few weeks, and then we can reassess," she said, meaning my upcoming appointment to have the lesion removed from my tongue.

The procedure didn't last long. Before I knew it, the spot was gone. The depression and crippling anxiety, however, were still very much with me!

For the next month, I had to eat liquid food and water, which didn't help my state of affairs. Neither did Christmas, because this was the first year that my mother didn't know it was my birthday. She'd always made the day special for me, giving me separate birthday gifts so I never felt cheated out of my day. But this year, she spent the holiday confined to her wheelchair, unaware of it being anything other than just another day. Her memories of me were just about gone.

"I can't stand the thought of looking
at you someday, this face I love,
and not knowing who you are."

Lisa Genova

Life went on. I begrudgingly took the meds I'd been prescribed, and hated it with every dosage. After my early years, I'd always hated drugs, but I hated being completely dependent on them even more. Up to this point in my life, I'd considered myself indestructible.

In the meantime, since we stopped dancing, Pam got busy and enrolled in the Geological Institute of America (GIA) to learn about precious stones. She wanted to make custom jewelry and sell it online. Pam earned her GIA certification and has been living her passion as a custom jeweler ever since.

I thought life couldn't get any worse for me, but then the time I'd been dreading for the past decade came: my mom lost her ten year battle with Alzheimer's.

I knew I was lucky, and told her often how I appreciated her unconditional love long before and long after her memory issues. She was a true leader who created a path for others to follow, loved her children unconditionally, was humble to a fault, and exemplified the most admirable work ethic. I thanked her for it all, all throughout my life.

I had no regrets when she died, except one: that I would no longer have the chance to sit next to her out in back of Patricia's house, overlooking the clear blue pool, watching the water lap back and forth, back and forth, basking in the sun shining down and in the memories I was able to keep for the both of us, and maybe – just maybe – catching one of her long lost smiles.

I'll say it to my very last breath: If there was a mom lottery, I won it.

Most of my mother's friends had made their transitions by now, but all of our friends attended her funeral to pay their respects. Patricia and I had a video made about her life's accomplishments, and it was impressive – even to me, even though I knew everything she'd done!

Her old boss George, who was instrumental in Mom's career at the bank, opened his eulogy by saying, "Beverly had fire engine red hair and a dynamic personality! We called her Showboat – not because she was a show-off, but because she was a high-performance stunner, and you couldn't help but stare in admiration every time she passed. Showboat never met a stranger, and she stayed humble and outworked others for her entire career. Even after she became the first female Vice President at the bank! She never, ever stopped."

As we laid Mom to rest, I read a poem I had written for her.

Pioneer Mother

My life is in turmoil, not sure what to do
The smell of dust and metal in the warehouse are way overdue
I established my own fate, but I didn't break
Because the stakes were too high for me to fly

I'm grateful you shared the sign of your time
Because the day I heard about your cancer, my mission changed
I would learn, grow, and reach higher than before
So, the next forty-five years would be my best encore

Many sunrises have passed since my decision
I thank you for being the catalyst to eliminate my indecision
At times I have felt uncertainty, but you have stood firm
Guiding us with your confidence, strength, and wisdom
Ultimately keeping me out of prison

We are thankful for your help to move us out of sight
For a chance to feel bright
You are proud of us, your children
We know because you told us so

How have we done Mother Beverly?

The first dame to rise to fame
At the bank with a star, you really went far
Becoming the first woman to achieve VP
Paving the way for other women to succeed

Forty-six years of leadership and hard work
Enabled you to travel the world and volunteer to help others
And for that you will be remembered by your sisters and brothers
As the well-spoken redhead who loved her family and friends and
All she greeted with that wonderful, vivacious smile

We never thought this time would come
Your special day in the sun
To shine and be reborn
With your father and mother in heaven

We love you unconditionally, our wonderful, loving Mother
You are the best Mom ever.

Just before her death, I'd come to the realization that I didn't want to rely on drugs anymore. I had just started researching natural supplements and holistic healing to replace my trips to the pharmacy and psychiatrist.

It was all coming together, and I actually felt empowered and in control of my mental health just before my mom died. But when she was gone, I quickly backslid once again into a depression.

I'm grateful she got to see my life turn around, and that she got to know Pam, but it shocked me how much I missed her. *I've been missing her for the past ten years*, I thought, *so maybe her death will be a blessing; I won't have to see her suffer anymore.*

Plus, might I remind you, I was a grown man! I thought I'd be well past my dependence on my mother, for goodness sakes.

But I was going to miss her listening to every word I said, her kindness, and the way she could ease my mind with just a few well-chosen words. I sure could use some right now.

Chapter Twenty-Three
The Comeback Kid

What would I tell my client if they came to me with the litany of issues I'm experiencing? I asked myself, considering my answer for a long time.

Well, I'd start by assuring them that life isn't easy, and there are a lot of ups and downs, but that we could work on the hard parts together. I'd assign them books to read, encourage them to meditate, and overhaul their diet. No more sugar for a while, limit caffeine, and – *aargh!* – stop drinking alcohol.

I decided to follow my own advice.

> *"If all that you're praying for is an easy life,*
> *what you're really praying for is the absence of life."*
>
> **Craig D. Lounsbrough**

If I wanted to change, I knew I had to make some uncomfortable, often painful changes in my daily life. But I quickly learned that bettering myself wasn't all about losing my perceived comforts, but finding unexpected joy and peace in my new patterns.

I joined a church that espoused a lot of the beliefs that were helping me through this period of depression and despair, which opened me up to new routines, interesting peers, and scintillating conversations.

Our church hosted many speakers, each expert on a diverse menu of topics that changed the way I looked at life. A very well-respected self-help practitioner named Terry, who had been through 30 surgeries to remove an E.coli infection caused by a defective spinal fusion procedure after a freak accident at work, shared his healing method during one of these sessions. To tell you that his talk moved me would be a grave understatement; it vibrated deep in my core, and something inside me clicked. I *had* to talk to him, and Pam and I managed to steal some of his time after his presentation.

"What you said that we are all divine beings that can create reality with our consciousness really resonated with us," I told him. And I don't know what came over me, but I welled up and told him about my mental breakdown. It felt like a release of sorts. I'm not sure if this makes sense, but I *knew* that *he* knew what to do with the information I'd just shared with him.

I was right. He listened intently to every word, nodded, and then asked, "Will you call me in the next couple of days? Here's my number..."

When we next chatted, he started off by saying, "From time to time, I coach people who I've randomly met if we share a connection. I feel strongly that you're in a prime position to receive the lessons I've learned along my journey. Would you like to be my student?"

I was flabbergasted. Just as I was about to ask how soon we could start, he said, "Oh, and this coaching is complimentary."

Immediately, I felt like The Comeback Kid.

> *"When you believe in someone, you profoundly increase their ability to have faith in themselves and achieve. When you love someone, you imprint on their heart something so powerful that it changes the trajectory of their life. When you do both, you set into motion, a gift to the world... because those who are believed in and loved understand the beauty of a legacy and the absolute duty of paying it forward."*
>
> **Jason Versey**

For the next several weeks, I absorbed Terry's life-changing process for healing.

One of the first things I began to learn was to be conscious of my incessant chatter and how negative it was. I realized the experiences, judgments, and stories I created from them are lies and are not ME. It was the first time I used visualization to get what I wanted.

All the while, I kept myself open to meeting new people with new ideas, exploring modalities I had never before experienced.

Pam and I happened to attend a meditation class at church on Sunday evening, led by a Buddhist monk who followed the teachings of Thích Nhất Hạnh. Ordained as a monk at age 16 in Vietnam, Thích Nhất Hạnh is credited with founding *engaged* Buddhism, which is simply applying ancient teachings to contemporary situations. You'd be surprised by how timeless the teachings remain! Engaged Buddhism believes in the complete yet complicated interdependence of all life, and the knowledge that we are all in this together. Its basis is that your sense of safety and calm is just as important as mine, and that leading with emphatic compassion brings awesome results. Thích Nhất Hạnh is known as the father of mindfulness, and dropped pearls of wisdom that I try to remember to repeat during meditations, like "Present moment, wonderful moment." His mindful communities were known as sanghas, and many were created around the world by his devotees.

Happily, there was even one in our Dallas church.

The sangha Pam and I joined was a happy, open-minded group of people with common interests centered on living a more fulfilling life, healing, loving, sharing, or simply meditating. Our sangha usually had around 20 to 30 people in attendance at any given time. Together, we learned sitting and walking meditations.

"Close your eyes...inhale and hold for one, two, three...now, exhale for one, two, three...focus on your breath, and only on your breath...can you feel your mind settle?"

It was difficult at first – as most new things tend to be – but it became almost natural over time.

After the meditation was complete, we sat in a circle and the sangha leader shared a story about current events, asking for feedback on the topic. I enjoyed the mediation, but Pam and I both believed that the socialization and mindfulness parts of the sangha were helping both of us cope with the stresses we were facing. Productive, eye-opening conversations should not be underestimated.

It didn't stop there. We tried other self-help modalities to complement the sangha including the Law of Attraction. The basis of this philosophy was that positive thoughts bring positive results, and that negative thoughts have an adverse effect. It almost sounded too good to be true and too easy, but it's a harder practice than it seems – especially when I had sunk into a dark hole of despair.

One Sunday, I met with a group from church to talk about healing. Everyone in attendance brought something to the table, but I remember Dan's share the most. He mentioned a book he had been reading about a triathlete who was hit while on his bicycle by a van traveling 40 miles per hour.

Dan told us that the triathlete was rushed to the hospital where he was told, "You have a broken back. I'm sorry, but you'll likely never walk again. There is one option, though..." The physician on duty detailed a radical surgery that included two steel rods in the triathlete's back.

"It's really the only choice," the doctor said.

"Nah," said the triathlete.

Instead, Dr. Joe Dispenza, the ill-fated triathlete who also happened to be a chiropractor, embarked on an adventure to heal himself through meditation and mental rehearsal. And then, after it worked, he wrote a book about it called *Evolve the Brain*.

Mental rehearsal is exactly what it sounds like: imagining performing a task as opposed to actual practicing it. Terry, during his coaching a year before, introduced me to visualization and is probably the reason I was more open to learning more. The idea is that if we visualize ourselves accomplishing a challenge or changing a habit, we improve our self-confidence, decrease our stress, and approach the actual challenge with a new, empowered mindset.

It's wild to read the studies. For example, subjects who mentally rehearsed one-handed piano exercises for two hours a day over a span of five days – without ever touching the piano keys – experienced almost the same level of proficiency as subjects who physically performed the same exercise on the piano. In another study, subjects who mentally rehearsed shooting basketballs from the free throw line were almost as proficient as the players who physically shot the basketball.

Subsequently, Dr. Joe released a second book called *Breaking the Habit of Being Yourself.* I studied that book from cover to cover, memorized the content, and made it part of me.

So when I heard he was hosting a two-day workshop in Austin, I knew that I had to attend. During a break the first day, I told Dr. Joe that I'd been trying to incorporate his methodology.

"I haven't been able to sit comfortably for months," I said. "I read your first book, and know that you rejected back surgery. I'm of the same mindset; I'll try anything to avoid surgery. That's why I'm here."

"I noticed that you had to stand up every so often during the morning presentation," he said. "Don't worry. By the time this workshop is over, you'll be able to heal yourself."

He wasn't kidding.

He held a guided meditation, and I was able to sit through it without having to stand to ease my back pain. It was as though the energy in the room from the others, with all of us sharing a singular focus of healing, powered me to sit through any pain I felt.

I told Pam later, "I think my mind has been playing tricks on me. I think I can handle this pain."

It felt like a lifetime ago when I told my doctor that I could no longer live with my pain. I didn't even recognize that me!

Dr. Joe had an intensive five-day workshop in Denver one month later, and I wasn't going to miss that one for anything. In it, we learned to practice his meditation and mental rehearsal exercise before the day became too hectic. I became so good at it that I was able to summarize his healing process into to three manageable steps to coach to others: preparation, creation, and ask.

Let me explain.

Step One involves preparation. It's not enough to say, "I want to be more successful" or "I want to lose weight and be healthier" or "I don't want to feel this debilitating pain anymore." You have to research the whys and hows behind the changes you wish to make until you are infallibly armed with knowledge and expertise. Next, find a quiet space, close your eyes, breathe deeply, and hold your breath for five to 15 seconds, after which you can exhale deeply. This is called pranic breathing. Repeat this sequence five or six times until your mind reaches a relaxed state of nothingness where your mind is still, and you're only focused on your breath. It may take some time to get used to this level of breathwork and focus.

Step Two is about creating the image you wish to achieve. As you rest in this place of nowhere, focusing on your breath, mentally rehearse the new behavior you want to adopt until it is firmly into your subconscious. Now, that place of nowhere is integral to your success in mental rehearsal; imagine it as a quiet, bottomless vessel emptied from all the noise in your life. We're consumed with incoming information from our Circle of Life including spiritual, family, work, finances, and pure strangers we meet along the way, adding their nonstop ideas and worries and stressors to our own. So, in carving out this sacred sanctuary of nowhere and nothingness, we create a safe space where we can become the best, updated version of ourselves. In that void, we're able to adopt new information and ways into our routines.

It's really the only way to break the patterns that hold us back.

Here's a simple, relatable example. Let's say that you want to reduce the anger that immediately pops up whenever a stressor enters your life.

It's the little moments, like when another driver steals the parking space for which you've been waiting patiently.

"Hey!" you yell impulsively, pounding on your horn. "What do you think you're doing?"

There are expletives, a shaking fist, but you move along and find another parking space.

Well done, you think afterwards. *I didn't get too out of hand. It's not like I punched the guy's lights out.*

But you're still shaking when you get out of your car, tense and easily annoyed afterward, and still angry a few hours later while retelling your partner what happened. If you think about it, that one moment has consumed the greater part of the day.

Wouldn't it be amazing to spend that time on something more productive? More positive? Instead of getting angry, recognize the old behavior in your meditation – "How dare someone cut in front of me! Didn't they see me?" – and change it in your mental rehearsal to, "In the grand scheme of life, it's not that important. I'll simply find another parking space." We can achieve that by creating a space in our mental rehearsal where the parking space, the discourteous driver, the sharp burst of reactive anger – none of it exist.

Here's the catch if you want to self improve: You must truly believe that whatever you want to change becomes more important than behaving in the old way.

Step Three is asking the universe to send you a sign that your request to change is on the right path, and acknowledging when it does. Observe when, where, and how the new behavior shows up in your life, then write down all the details surrounding this new behavior so that you have recorded proof that your mental rehearsals are indeed working.

Continue journaling until you have fully inserted the new program into your subconscious.

In a nutshell, that's PCA: preparation, creation, and ask/acknowledge. Catchy, isn't it?

This methodology didn't remove all my stressors completely. Life is, after all, a series of hopeful attempts followed by a series of both failures and triumphs. Sure, we hope like heck for the easy parts, but the lows are valuable, too.

Remember that tongue lesion I had removed? It came back when I experienced more stress related to my mother's death and our move to Orange County. My first reaction was, "Oh, no! Not again!" But I quickly fell into my new PCA habits, reprogrammed my subconscious, and learned how to better deal with my stress. And – poof! – that lesion disappeared.

I practiced PCA until it became second nature, and the progress in my life continued to expand. My costochondritis healed. I started driving again, exercising, and relearning my dance steps. One by one, I shed my stressors.

For old time's sake, Pam and I competed in The Gumbo Classic in Baton Rouge against an impressive roster of competitors. We ended up winning the Senior Latin division before finally retiring our competitive dance shoes, which made for one heck of a last hurrah!

Note: We still cut a rug whenever we catch some Latin music!

Professionally, my coaching business continued to reap rewards, both financially and emotionally. I also enjoyed my volunteer work with SCORE where I mentored founders and entrepreneurs. Showing others their own paths to success and career fulfillment had a real impact on me, and I never tired of sharing my expertise.

The Comeback Kid was back in business!

Whenever I explained to someone how I'd been in their same stuck position at a few points in my life, they'd always ask, "You? Really? Well, how did you make it back?"

I loved that question because it allowed me to share how I moved my mental health into remission and helped all other areas of my life to thrive, and it reminded me of how I'd changed so much. It was because of that question, and specifically for my clients and mentees, that I designed the Comeback Wheel.

Comeback Wheel Figure 2.

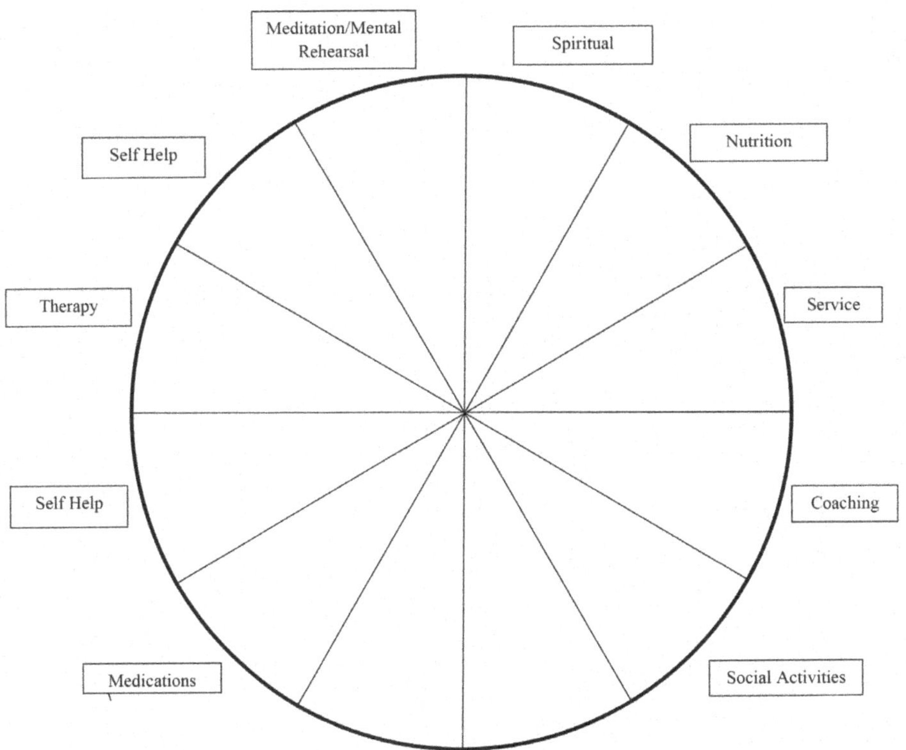

Whether we admit it or not, the best pies are the ones that are shared with others, with everyone enjoying the same size piece. Now, if there's a cherry pie in front of me, I might disagree with the whole sharing equally concept and want to eat the entire thing...but I know that wouldn't be healthy for me.

That same philosophy applies to our unique areas of fulfillment, too. If we look at our pie – or, our life – as one giant piece that we greedily keep to ourselves, we won't be able to participate in it fully or effectively.

Let me explain. If my only focus is on accumulating wealth, and I only say yes to things if they guarantee income (and a lot of it), and spend all of my time counting my money...then what?

No, really. Then what? My answer is that I cannot imagine a more meaningless existence. And I really like money!

The secret to my Comeback Wheel is that every area that can better your time on Earth should be equally apportioned and served up regularly. Using the sections above and tweaking them to your own hierarchy of needs, you can create a pie that will feed you for the rest of your life.

For me, joining and participating in a church enabled me to feel closer to Spirit, while fulfilling my payback for all the prosperity the Higher Authority has bestowed upon me.

Coaching helped me find my purpose in life, to help people improve their performance and create never-ending cycles of prosperity.

Through exercise and dancing, I improved my health and expanded my social happiness and satisfaction at the same time.

I can't rule out the positive effect medications had on my survivability; without them, I wouldn't have achieved the clarity and calm I needed to change my patterns.

And then there's meditation and the mental rehearsal I've incorporated into my daily life before my day gets hectic. This simple yet highly effective practice helps me move into the present moment from the unproductive past, and create the new me. It's one of the most crucial parts of the Comeback Wheel, and keeps the whole thing moving.

By revamping my nutrition, I allowed my body the physical ability to handle incoming stress purely. I eliminated processed foods and oils, stopped drinking alcohol and caffeine, and dropped sugar.

One of the most important lessons I incorporated was to seek help wherever and whenever I could find it, from pranic healing and local support groups, to attending expert seminars and reading books by those who had already been there, done that, and lived to tell the tale.

Service has always and will always be a significant part of my life because it sets up an environment of sharing, caring, and the empowerment of others.

Of course, we all need to let off steam and socialize. Between dancing, church, and my business organizations, I enjoyed interactions daily that fed my mind, body, and soul.

I was also fortunate enough to experience the benefits of therapy and, specifically, Cognitive Behavior Therapy (CBT). In the simplest of explanations, CBT is talking therapy that lays out thought records of how I handled situations in the past, and illustrates how disordered and distorted my thought were when I was depressed and anxious. By changing the way I think and behave, CBT has opened a world of possibilities to better manage my problems effectively and positively.

As my old mentor, John, once advised me, it's important to find your purpose in life by aligning yourself with what you value most. But what he didn't tell me is that a life purpose can shift over time.

Now, I want to be of service to others and stay true to my spiritual commitment. I lead with gratitude and love.

And if I ever start feeling out of whack, I check back in with the Comeback Wheel. Are all my slices equal? Are they all still delicious to me? And, finally, am I leading with gratitude and a servant attitude?

It always does the trick.

Chapter Twenty-Four
Dance Like Everyone's Watching!

"You talk a lot about how ballroom dancing has a positive effect on Alzheimer's patients," asked someone in the audience. "But why are you the only one talking about it?"

I'll never forget that moment. I'd just given my first speech to a group on Catalina Island about a study focused on the health benefits of ballroom dancing, and how I and many others were intent on changing the fate of Alzheimer's patients from despair to hope.

> *"You can't answer a question without being confronted by another question. The answer to that next question is what brings improvement."*
>
> **Aniekee Tochukwu Ezekiel**

"I...don't know," I stuttered. "But I'm going to find out."

My Catalina speech centered on a 21-year study titled *Leisure Activities and the Risk of Dementia in the Elderly*, the results of which were published in the New England Journal of Medicine in 2003. In it, they measured the rate at which at-risk seniors progressed in their Alzheimer's journeys while participating in therapeutic activities like reading, writing, playing a musical instrument, and 11 physical activities like dancing, walking, and swimming.

The surprise of the study was that the only physical activity offering any protection against the risk of Alzheimer's and cognitive decline was dancing.

Dancing! Yes, the theory is that dancing is a multi-modal exercise, meaning participants rise, fall, twist, and turn, move front to back and side to side, dancing with a partner, all while listening to music. The physical intimacy required in partner dancing is therapeutic, too, demanding that partners communicate effectively to learn new steps, retain balance, and synchronize their body movements. Couples also learn conflict resolution because they must negotiate more effectively when disagreements emerge on the dance floor.

As you know by now, dance and Alzheimer's both had a significant impact on my life. Pam and I met ballroom dancing, and we were a successful duo on the competitive circuit for many years. As for Alzheimer's, my mother spent ten years trying to hold on to her memories until she ultimately succumbed to the ravages of the disease. We have seen – up close and personal – the emotional wear and financial cost of this all-consuming disease.

Today there are six million people with dementia whose treatment and care exceed $200 billion, making it second in financial devastation to heart disease. In the next several years, it is estimated dementia will cost over $1 trillion in care, becoming the most expensive disease to treat in the United States.

Immediately on my return home from Catalina, I looked at that study again. Joe Verghese was the first doctor listed on the abstract, so I called his office the next morning to set up a time to talk.

When we finally linked up, I asked him, "Why hasn't the medical community promoted the health benefits of social dancing if it's so good for you, and especially for Alzheimer's patients?"

"Lack of funding," he said without hesitation. "Most grants go to Big Pharma clinical trials – not social studies about the benefits of dancing."

> *"If you want to make unique discoveries, you do not follow the crowd."*
>
> **Steven Magee**

After a few phone conversations with Dr. Verghese, I went to visit him at the Albert Einstein College of Medicine in New York. He's an expert on aging who assesses how diseases and aging affect cognitive ability and mobility in older adults. I was shocked to learn that his own mother also died from complications related to Alzheimer's, but it let me know that this trial was near and dear to his heart.

We came away from the meeting with Dr. Joe very impressed; his world-class credentials, facilities, and team, as well as his authenticity and sincerity made an impact on us, and we were immediately ready to partner with him.

I couldn't persuade USA Dance, who had thousands of members across the country, to participate in fundraising, so I decided to raise the money for the research on my own.

My non-profit, The Beverly McCombs Foundation – Dance for Cognitive Enhancement, partnered with the Orange County USA Dance chapter, and held our first formal fundraising event at the Richard M. Nixon Library in Yorba Linda, California. It was a feast for the senses between the classical music playing in the background, the mouth-watering aromas wafting from the kitchens, and beauty everywhere your eyes happened to land. The women were dressed in ball gowns of every color, the men fitted in nicely pressed tuxedos and suits. Peppered throughout the venue were dance hosts strategically positioned to ask single men and women if they would like to dance. It was beyond charming, it was stunning!

Near the entrance to the formal ballroom, we'd set up a silent auction where patrons bid on experiences like a sailing adventure, classical guitar lessons, and a stay at the luxe Montage Resort in Laguna Beach. Everyone seemed to have their own style of competitive bidding, and it was fun to see how secretive and sly they tried to be!

When the East Room doors opened for dancing after dinner, a flood of over 200 patrons spilled onto the beautiful terrazzo ballroom dance floor alit by the grand crystal chandeliers. That's when the real party began, with lively dancing and drinking to raucous big band music.

Linda, our chairwoman, asked her dance studio to persuade Louis Van Amstel, one of the biggest, most talented personalities from the popular television show Dancing With the Stars, to be our celebrity guest. He danced with several star-struck women, demonstrating that he still had the dance moves that put him atop the ballroom dance world as a professional ballroom dancer.

No one wanted to leave! The only way the night ended was for us to politely ask the remaining dancing enthusiasts to vacate the dance floor so that the Nixon Library cleaners could clean up and get home at a reasonable hour!

I started my non-profit foundation in my mother's name to accept the donations from the night at the Nixon, along with all subsequent donations the foundation would receive. After several years of our fund-raising as well as the award of a federal grant, Dr. Verghese was able to start a new study called *Movement Intervention and Memory Enhancement (MIME).*

Rhythm Brakes Cares (RBCares), based in New York City, partnered with Dr. Verghese and my foundation to provide instruction for participants in the dancing cohort for the MIME research. RBCares' mission is to provide the restorative power of music, movement, and touch to older adults with dementia. Since 2009, RBCares has offered their love and knowledge of dance to improve the quality of life for those with all stages of dementia residing in the community or in a memory care facility. RBCares dance artists are professionally trained ballroom and modern dancers who have completed training to work with older adults with dementia.

MIME started June 2019 with 32 randomly selected seniors 65 and older, comparing social dancing to a walking exercise. Participants were hooked up to MRI machines to monitor and measure any changes in the memory centers of the brain.

The outcome was incredible! It clearly demonstrated how social dancing protected against the risk of cognitive decline in the dancing cohort versus the walking exercise, and these results hopefully will be published in high profile journal. Furthermore, Dr. Verghese is gearing up to conduct an even larger MIME study.

To date, 99.5% of clinical trials to find a cure for dementia have failed. Those aren't great odds, are they?

But I remain my mother's son, living out her life motto when it comes to changing the fate of an Alzheimer's diagnosis. I will stay humble and be the hardest worker in the room trying to change the face of Alzheimer's through dance.

Chapter Twenty-Five
All You Need is Love

"Hey, brother," Patricia would taunt. "Why don't you put on a shirt that fits?"

My sister loved nothing more than to tease me mercilessly. When I was five years old, that wasn't terribly fun. It still wasn't fun through high school and college, but I eventually got used to it and understood that razzing me was her love language.

So, apparently, was bossing me around!

> *"A sister is a dearest friend, a closest enemy, and an angel at the time of need."*
>
> **Debasish Mridha**

But just when I'd begin to lose my temper with her antics, she'd break into her favorite song, and I'd soften a little.

"There's nothin' you can do that can't be done..." she'd croon. "Nothin' you can sing that can't be sung...Nothin' you can say, but you can learn how to play the game...It's easy..."

According to Patricia, all you needed was love. She was the type of person who wouldn't hurt a flea – literally! If she saw a bug in the house, she'd carefully cover it with a glass, slide a piece of paper under it, and escort the bug outside to a safe location where she thought it could make a new life for itself.

"Nothin' you can make that can't be made...No one you can save that can't be saved...Nothin' you can do, but you can learn how to be you in time...It's easy..."

After her infamous night in jail during college, she spent the next 34 years in sobriety with Alcoholics Anonymous. When my mother was diagnosed with Alzheimer's, she helped found the Dallas chapter to spread awareness about the disease, offer support, and fundraise to find a cure. Her energy and care for other families going through the pain of watching a loved one disappear before their very eyes was endless and beautiful.

She also loved to remodel houses. When our mother's memory issues accelerated, she and her husband bought a bigger house, and worked their tails off to update it so Mom could live out the rest of her life comfortably.

She was one of the most hardworking, impressive people I was lucky enough to know.

If I had to choose one memory that perfectly illustrated our relationship, I'd pick the time we canoed down the Guadalupe River during our college years in Austin. I was seated in the front, and Patricia was behind me. All I heard for the entire canoe ride was, "You're rowing too slowly!" and then, "Too fast, Bruce!" and then, "WHAT ARE YOU DOING?" as we zigged and zagged for miles.

"Just follow my strokes!" I yelled.

"Why would I do that?!" Patricia yelled back. "I'm the one who's canoed before! You haven't!"

Oy. My apologies to any hikers, wildlife, or fauna that heard our colorful language that afternoon.

We eventually got so fed up with each other that we steered to shore, got out of that God-forsaken canoe, dragged it on land, and left it there for someone else to pick up. Then we stomped back to our campsite mad as hornets, not saying one word to each other for a very long time.

And then wouldn't you know it, Patricia broke into song. "All you need is love! All you need is love! All you need is love, love...Love is all you need..."

We both busted out laughing.

My sister sure lived by those lyrics until she died after a fierce battle with cancer. At her memorial service, we played her favorite Beatles songs, and everyone sang along in her spirit.

"There's nothin' you can know that isn't known...Nothin' you can see that isn't shown...There's nowhere you can be that isn't where you're meant to be...It's easy..."

I can't hear that song without thinking of her. She lived by its lyrics from the moment that song was released. Now that she's gone, she continues to live on through them. What a legacy she leaves.

> *"You may be as different as the sun and the moon, but the same blood flows through both your hearts. You need her, as she needs you..."*
>
> **George R.R. Martin**

I spoke with her friends and acquaintances at her memorial, all equally gutted by the loss of her in their lives. One friend who she sponsored in AA told me, "Whenever I had the urge to drink again, Patricia was there encouraging me to stay with AA's program. I want you to know that your sister saved my life."

She routinely saved mine, too. Patricia is the one who introduced me to many of the self-help gurus that opened my eyes to new ideas and changed my patterns. I often poked fun at her big theory questions, but she got me asking things like, "Who am I?" and "What's my purpose in this lifetime?"

The answers I found were because of her.

Unlike with my mother, I definitely had regrets about my relationship with Patricia. While there were definitely copious amounts of caring, kindness, listening, understanding, and compassion between us, I was often unable to show the same level of love and affection as she demonstrated effusively toward me.

I think I was just way too angry growing up without a father, and that bitterness carried over in the way I expresssed emotion. God forbid I let someone in to witness my vulnerability or my deep desire to be loved unconditionally!

None of that seemed to matter to Patricia, though. All she needed was love, and she knew in her heart that she had mine. I didn't need to be anyone I couldn't be, and, in fact, I didn't need to be anyone but her little brother.

When she was nearing her end here on Earth, I flew to Dallas from Orange County to help care for her. As soon as she saw me, the expression on her face was so bright that it rivaled the sun.

"You're here to rescue me!" she exclaimed, beaming up at me from her wheelchair and reaching for my arm. As she nuzzled into me, I heard her utter her lifelong mantra.

"All you need is love."

In a heartbeat, I forgot all about my fear of vulnerability, and any bravado I had left melted away.

"I love you," I told her, first quietly and then with all the feeling in my heart. "I LOVE YOU, PATRICIA."

And if I thought the smile on her face when she saw me was pure sunshine, the smile she gave me when I finally expressed my love for her was more like a vibrant rainbow that only comes out after a really good rain.

It was fitting that her very last words when she finally transitioned were a whispered, "All you need is love."

I can't imagine needing anything else.

It isn't lost on me that the women in my life had a profound effect on the man I am today. Starting with my grandmother, who informed me regularly that I was just like my father – and not in a good way!

For far too long, I let myself believe her words. For too long, I gave her opinion of him far more weight than my own opinion of myself.

I wish I'd have had the confidence to respond to her constant criticism. I wish I would've told her, "Oh, really? That's hard to believe. Never met the guy."

When I finally did meet him, I found him to be a fine person. Did I approve of the way he turned his back on my mother and his children? Certainly not. Would I have acted the same way, given similar circumstances? Certainly not. I can look back at my life and know that one for certain.

But everyone has a moment or two when they didn't live up to their own standards. I certainly do.

When my grandmother left this life, I felt lighter than I'd ever felt before. Sure, I was sad that she passed, but it was such a weight off my shoulders; she'd placed my father on my back, and forced me to carry him with me all those years.

The other woman who changed the trajectory of my life more than a few times was, of course, my mother. She was my anchor, the wind in my sails, my GPS in life and business, and my warning alarm that kept me from sinking many, many times. She gave me the best life she possibly could, taught me that success is the self-fulfillment for the benefit of others, and left me with a legacy that still astounds me.

And then there was Patricia, my partner-in-crime who taught me how to love and feel worthy of love.

Which brings me to my living dream, Pam. She's everything I'd been missing in my life, and I wake up every morning and fall asleep with the same gratitude prayer: "Thank you for my beautiful wife and for sending her to me."

I fought my whole life to find her, preparing for the day I finally did. I said yes to dance lessons, I said no to undervaluing myself, and I said, "Heck yeah!" when I saw her on the crowded dance floor.

Someone recently asked me, "Don't you wish you found each other sooner?"

I think about that a lot. Yes, I wish for nothing more than extra time with her, but I honestly wouldn't have been ready for her in my twenties, thirties, or even my early forties.

Trust the timing of your dreams. They'll never let you down.

So, I'd like to thank the women in my life for making me the man I am today: someone who knows that the very best way to be happy on Mondays is to create a life you can't wait to wake up and live.

Book Review

Thank you for reading my book,
How to Be Happy on Mondays.
I know you had many options,
but you read this one and for that I am grateful.

I hope that it added value to your life
and helped in some way.
Your feedback is important and
hope that you can take some time to post a review.

Appreciate your support,
and wish you continued success! .

Made in USA - Kendallville, IN
27326_9781944066994
06.18.2022 1315